The 4-1-1 on Reinventing You

Open Pages Publishing, LLC

Open Pages Publishing, LLC
Estero, FL 33906
http://www.my411books.com/contact/open-pages-publishing
(239) 454-7700

© 2016 Michele Sfakianos, RN, BSN
All rights reserved

No part of this book may be reproduced or transmitted in any form or by any means, electronic or mechanical, including photocopying, recording, or by any information storage, and retrieval system, without written permission from the author or publisher.

ISBN: 978-0-9960687-7-2 • Paperback
ISBN: 978-0-9960687-8-9 • Ebook
Library of Congress Control Number: 2016911786

Printed in the United States of America

Because of the dynamic nature of the Internet, any Web addresses or links contained in this book may have changed since publication and may no longer be valid. The views expressed in this work are solely those of the author and do not necessarily reflect the views of the publisher, and the publisher hereby disclaims any responsibility for them.

Author/Book website: http://www.my411books.com
Coach & Speaking website: http://www.takeactionwithmichele.com

Disclaimer

The information in this book is:
- of a general nature and not intended to address the specific circumstances of any particular individual or entity;
- written as a guide and is not intended to be a comprehensive tool, but is complete, accurate, or up to date at the time of writing;
- an information tool only and not intended to be used in place of a visit, consultation, or advice of a medical professional;

This book is not intended to serve as professional or legal advice (if you need specific advice, you should always consult a suitably qualified professional).

Dedication

. . . .

*No matter what stage of life you are in, this book is for you.
It's never too late to find your calling and reinvent yourself!*

Table of Contents

Acknowledgements ix
Introduction xi

Chapter 1: What's My Purpose?. 1
Chapter 2: Get Out of Your Own Way!. 9
Chapter 3: Changing Self-Talk 15
Chapter 4: Are You Up for the Challenge?. 23
Chapter 5: Going Back to School?. 29
Chapter 6: Who's Your Mentor?. 35
Chapter 7: Take Time to Declutter 43
Chapter 8: Be Grateful. 51
Chapter 9: Step Out in Faith. 57
Chapter 10: Creating Goals. 65
Chapter 11: Words Create Realities 77
Chapter 12: Affirmations and Visualizations. 87
Chapter 13: Networking and Social Media 95
Chapter 14: Transformation Requires Self-Care. 103

Conclusion. 107
Resources 111
Index 113
About the Author. 117

Acknowledgements

Thank you to everyone who continues to support my writing. Without your thirst for knowledge and your incredible faith in me, I would not have been challenged to write. I am fortunate to live my purpose, through my passion, to help others.

Thank you to my family and friends for encouraging me to share my knowledge. Through this information, I want you to live the life you were called to live.

Introduction

There is a lot of chatter today about reinventing yourself, especially after 50. There's no "magical" age when you find yourself in a difficult situation, whether it be a divorce, death of a loved one, or a job loss, and have to make some tough decisions. It is these times that you need to re-evaluate your life and determine the best path for you. You can't listen to others advice on what you "should" do with your life. It's your life, do with it what you want. When it is all said and done, what do you want to be said at your funeral? Do you want people to talk about your life contributions or the fact that you listened to everyone else and did things that you didn't even enjoy? Do you want them to talk about how happy you lived, or how sad you always seemed to be?

Making real, deep, lasting change in your life is hard work. It requires diligence, commitment, a willingness to take risks and the nerve to summon the reserves of inner strength you don't know you have. Deciding to take on a new career can be hard. There is something new to learn; new people to meet; perhaps courses to take; all while trying to figure out how you will continue to pay your monthly bills. Don't get discouraged. I want you to know that I've reinvented myself several times and, although hard, has been the most rewarding part of my journey so far.

After graduating high school, the field of technology was beginning to take off, so I decided to get a degree in Computer Programming. It wasn't an easy field to enter after graduation, since no one would hire a pregnant woman! When I returned to the workforce, I was able to get jobs similar to the field with the Accounting background I had, but no programming jobs. The technology field changes quickly and it was too difficult at the time to keep up with the changes, so I just took the jobs I could get. Talk about the feeling of defeat!

Six years later, I got a divorce and was faced with the dilemma of raising two small children and although I did get child support, the thought of how I was going to pay my bills was overwhelming. I picked up the newspaper one day to see what the highest paying jobs were, and I found Nursing to be the winner! Hence – reinvention #1. I contacted the local college to see how

The 4-1-1 on Reinventing You

many of my existing credits from my previous degree would transfer, spoke to my mom about moving in with her temporarily, and took the plunge. I worked three part-time jobs; went to school full-time; and took care of two small children. No easy feat – but I did it in under three years.

I worked in various Nursing positions throughout the years – floor nurse, Nurse Recruiter and then into Informatics Nursing. Informatics Nursing is where I landed for over twenty years. I was finally able to utilize my Computer Programming Degree, along with my Nursing Degree, to build clinical systems for hospital staff. The best part about this job was I was able to work from home.

While working from home, I completed the course work to become a Certified Legal Nurse Consultant and also received a Real Estate License. Could this be reinvention #2 – perhaps not, but I have the additional certification and license in case I want to do something else.

In the meantime, I discovered my passion for writing. I loved writing so much that I wrote and self-published ten books, all while still working full-time. I was always looking for other ways to utilize my writing skills and it was at that time I realized that I had a wonderful message I could be sharing with others. Now – reinvention #2. I learned about a Certification program, offered by John Maxwell – the #1 Leadership Guru in the world, and felt a new calling to take this Certification and open a new business. This new business would allow me to be a Coach, Speaker and Trainer – all while having my own content (books) and the new content (John Maxwell's) to share. I refer to myself as a Life Transformation Specialist because I help people to "grow forward" in their purpose and vision for their life. I help them to find the answers within themselves to transform their life to the life they desire. I completed this Certification in my early fifties and couldn't be happier.

So you see, it doesn't matter what age you are, with the right guidance and proven steps, you can take on that career or personal change and be the person you were born to be. The chapters in this book are a proven stepping stone to your reinvention, no matter how big or how small.

> *"To be yourself in a world that is constantly trying to make you something else is the greatest accomplishment."*
> —Ralph Waldo Emerson

Chapter One

What's My Purpose?

• • • • • • • • • • • • • • •

"You're never too old to set another goal or dream a new dream."
—C. S. Lewis

Are you feeling unmotivated, unsure of yourself, aimless, can't find your passion, directionless, not clear on what your purpose in life is? You're in good company — most people are in the same boat.

Many think their purpose should be obvious and easy to identify, an idea that leads to much frustration and disappointment. More typically your purpose will slowly emerge as you put one foot in front of the other, following where your heart, talents and life seem to be leading you.

You may even go through a season where you long to find it, to the point that you feel deep emotional pain but can't seem to find a clue anywhere. If you have this experience, like I did, you could even start believing that everyone else might have a purpose, but you very sadly don't.

There may be the occasional person who knows their purpose from the time they were a child, sets out on the perfect course of study, and spends their whole life doing what they were meant to. This wasn't my experience, and chances are it's not yours either.

As you go through this journey, gaining wisdom about yourself and receiving exciting, surprising clues from life (similar to a treasure hunt), your sense of purpose will evolve and change.

After I left Nursing, I envisioned my life as a speaker and writer. I started publishing books, and speaking on Life Skills, Parenting and Raising

The 4-1-1 on Reinventing You

Teenagers. Then I discovered a passion for coaching, for helping people to transform their life and discover their purpose to create a more fulfilling, happier life.

> **Learn to get out of your own way.**

At each phase I thought I had found my purpose and it felt like – and looked like – I kept changing my mind. I never imagined that one day I would find my ultimate purpose in merging all of the above to serve others. Today, I speak about creating a healthier, happier, more fulfilling life (public speaking). There's usually a book signing after (writing), and at that time people who want to work with me will sign up for one-on-one programs (coaching aka life transformation).

It may have looked like I kept changing my mind and was trying to create several careers at once, which is generally a bad idea. My purpose was simply evolving as I explored each area, acquiring the skills and experience that would end up creating the whole pie.

Now, there about a million things online telling you how to find your passion in life, and that's a good thing. It's a search worth undergoing. There is no one-way to find your passion – learn to get out of your own way. We will discuss more of this in Chapter 2. For now, we will refer to this as "getting out of your box."

Your personal box is the small world you live in, where you are the center of the universe. You are concerned with your wellbeing, with not wanting to look bad, with succeeding in life, with your personal pleasure (good food, good music, good relationships, good career, etc.).

When someone tells you that you look fat, this only hurts because you're in your personal box. You take that statement and believe that it's about you, and feel the pain or embarrassment of how the statement affects you. It matters a lot, because in your box, what matters most is how everything affects you personally.

Some other problems caused by this personal box:
- In our box, we're concerned with our pleasure and comfort, and try not to be uncomfortable. This is why we don't exercise, why we don't eat healthy food.
- This fear of being uncomfortable is why we get anxious at the thought of meeting strangers. It hampers our social life and our love life.

What's My Purpose?

- Because we don't want to look bad, we are afraid of failing. So we don't tackle tough things.
- We procrastinate because of this fear of failing, this fear of discomfort.
- When someone does or says something, we relate that event with how it affects us, and this can cause anger or pain or irritation.
- We expect people to try to give us what we want, and when they don't, we get frustrated or angry.

Actually, pretty much all our problems are caused by this box.

If we can learn to get outside this personal box, and see things from a less self-centered approach, we can see some amazing things:

- When someone says or does something, it's not really about us — it's about pain or fear or confusion they're feeling, or a desire they have. Not us.
- When we have an urge for temporary pleasure (TV, social media, junk food), we can see that this urge is a simple passing physical sensation, and not the center of the universe.
- We can start to see that our personal desires are actually pretty trivial, and that there's more to life than trying to meet our pleasures and shy from our discomfort. There's more than our little fears including the pain and suffering of other people, and compassion for them.
- We can tie our daily actions, like learning about how our minds and bodies and habits work, or getting healthy, or creating something, not only to our personal satisfaction and success but to how they help others, how they make the lives of others better, and how they might lessen the suffering of others.

We become less self-centered, and begin to have a wider view. Everything changes, from letting go of fear and anger and procrastination, to changing our habits and finding work that matters.

Once we get out of the box, and see things with a wider view, we can start a journey along a path like this:

1. We can start to see the needs of others, and feel for their suffering.
2. We work to make their lives better, and lessen their suffering.
3. Even if we aren't good at that, we can learn skills that help us to be better at it. It's the intention that matters.

The 4-1-1 on Reinventing You . . . .

   4. As we go about our daily work, we can tie our actions to this greater purpose. Learning a program or becoming healthy, for example, isn't just for our betterment, but for the betterment of others, even in a small way. This gives us motivation on a moment-to-moment basis. When we lose motivation, we need to get back out of our box, shed our concern for our discomfort and fears, and tie ourselves to a bigger purpose.

What matters is becoming bigger than yourself. Once you do, you learn that you have a purpose in life.

Sounds great right? Getting outside this personal box isn't easy. It takes work.

   1. You must see when you're stuck in the box. Whenever you're angry, frustrated, irritated, fearful, anxious, procrastinating, feeling hurt, wishing people would be different ... you're in the box. When you can't stick to habits, or have a hard time with a diet, you're in the box. Your momentary pleasure is what matters in this box.
   2. When you notice that you're in the box, expand your mind and heart. See the bigger picture. Feel what others are feeling. Try to understand rather than condemning. See how little and petty your concerns and fears have been. Realize that if others treat you badly, it's not about you, but about their suffering.
   3. Always wish others well. Genuinely want their happiness, just as you want your own happiness. See their suffering and wish for it to end or lessen.
   4. Offer help to others. How can you lessen the suffering of others? Sometimes it's just by paying attention, just listening. Other times you just need to be there, just lend a hand. You don't need to go around solving everyone's problems — they probably don't want that. Just be there for them.

By all means set out on the course that feels and seems right to you, but be open to learning from it and adjusting. What experience or purpose is calling to you? Give it a chance. If it causes you to change your mind or even abandon what you sincerely thought was the right path for you, you're wiser for having tried it. You'll learn to be bigger than yourself. You'll learn that the life we've been given is a gift, and we must make the most of it, and

What's My Purpose?

not waste a second. You'll learn that there is nothing more fulfilling than making the lives of others a little better.

> **Your life purpose is your intention, based on and aligned with your values and your principles.**

Don't get too stressed about this or put too much pressure on yourself about clarifying your purpose. Your purpose might indeed be something grand and complicated, or it may be as simple as dispensing love and kindness wherever you go. Remember to be present in the moment, and delight in watching it all unfold. Life really is beautiful. Your life purpose is your intention, based on and aligned with your values and your principles.

Now that you're out of your box, let's move on to getting out of our own way. I've been told many times that God determines our destiny, but we determine the steps to get there, so get stepping!

The 4-1-1 on Reinventing You . . . .

Self-Discovery Challenge:

If you had to leave the house all day, every day, where would you go and what would you do? Or, what's the one thing I love doing so much, I would gladly do it for free? *What most people don't understand is that passion is the result of action, not the cause of it.*

What would your perfect day look like? Describe every detail.

What activities set your soul on fire?

. . . . **What's My Purpose?**

Connect with your inner child:

What brought you immense joy as a kid?

What were you doing when you lost track of time?

What did your parents have to drag you away from?

The 4-1-1 on Reinventing You . . . .

What did you love deep down before the world told you to get practical?

Chapter Two

Get Out of Your Own Way!

"There is nothing more dreadful than the habit of doubt. Doubt separates people. It is a poison that disintegrates friendships and breaks up pleasant relations. It is a thorn that irritates and hurts; it is a sword that kills."
—Gautama Buddha

Day after day we get stuck in a vicious cycle. We are stuck in false relationships, dead-end jobs, or stuck in a body that doesn't suit our liking. Are you stuck in old habits, unproductive patterns, or lifestyles that hinder your pathway to joy?

You probably have plenty of reasons why you don't get things done. Many of them are outside of your control. But instead of focusing on things you can't control, focus on the biggest barrier, the one which you have the most control over: You.

You're probably standing in your own way, so here are 15 things that will help you get out of your own way. Even if you do only five of the steps, you'll finally be able to get things done. When it comes to accomplishing my big goals, it's not everything else that is the problem—it's me. At times, I am my own worst enemy.

1. **Remember why you are doing it.** Knowing why you are doing something is critical to getting it done. Humans hate doing things for no reason. Whether it's washing the dishes, starting a business or filling out job applications, it must contribute to some larger purpose. If it doesn't, quit doing it.

The 4-1-1 on Reinventing You

2. **Think about the outcome.** What are you going to get from doing this thing? When you don't feel like doing it, focus on the outcome you're seeking. Think about how that outcome will make your life better, no matter how big or small the improvement. If that outcome doesn't excite you, that's probably why you aren't doing it. Cross it off the list.

3. **Focus on the important stuff.** Nothing will drain your energy faster than working on or putting off tedious things that won't move you toward your goal. For example, if you're starting a business, stop moving commas and periods around in your business plan and go out and talk to some prospects. Sell something or get feedback to improve. Focusing on what will make a difference will motivate you and skyrocket your results.

4. **Listen to music.** There's a reason music is so popular. It has a huge effect on how you feel. Use it as a tool to change your mood to whatever you want it to be. Create a playlist of songs that motivates everything in you. Play it while you work and while you procrastinate.

5. **When you get tired, move around.** Do some jumping jacks, some simple exercises, or (my personal favorite) just dance like no one is watching for a few minutes. Despite common beliefs, you actually get energy from being active. Your body did not evolve to sit at a computer and work for hours at a time. You can do it, but you have to work to create the energy. Combine with point #4 for accelerated results.

6. **When you get frustrated, meditate.** You're probably thinking too much. Calm down. Sit in a comfortable spot, relax and take some deep breaths to clear your mind for 10 minutes. If you really want to boost your productivity, meditate before you get frustrated in order to keep your mind clear, stay relaxed and avoid the frustration that stops you from getting things done. *See Chapter 12 for more on meditation.

7. **Forget failure.** You can't have success without failure. Yeah, yeah, you've heard it before.... So why do we worry about failing when we know it's a necessary part of the process? Do your best to expect failure, and try even harder to learn from it.

8. **Be consistent.** Consistency will keep you going; unfailing hard work will help maintain the momentum you created by first pulling the trigger. "We are what we repeatedly do," Aristotle once said. "Excellence, then, is not an act, but a habit."

9. **Choose your friends wisely.** You know the saying "you are what you eat." Well it's also true when it comes to who you keep company with. Are you running with the right crowd? Because the people you interact with on a daily basis directly influence who you are and what you do. Make sure you surround yourself with people who encourage you and hold you accountable—people who you can learn positive habits from.

10. **Systematize everything.** On average an adult makes roughly 35,000 decisions a day. No wonder we stall out when it comes to getting started on our goals. Systematizing your processes takes decision-making out of the process, leaving more mental room for bigger and better thinking.

11. **Reflect on your influence.** Ask yourself how the work you do affects others. We all transform other people whether we're conscious of it or not—so really think about how you'll be helping someone else for a little motivation. By working on your goal or project, you could spur someone else to pull the trigger on theirs. You just have to pull your trigger first.

12. **Stop comparing yourself to other people.** You know the feeling. You're working on something and you suddenly stop in despair because you realize it's not going to be as good as [insert celebrity, colleague, friend, or relative] would do it. It stops you in your tracks. You say to yourself, "Why bother? It's going to suck anyway." First, this is not true. You are just as good or better than that person. Second, even if you can't do it as well as that person, no problem. This is practice to make you better. Either way, there's no reason to stop.

13. **Give up the ridiculous idea of perfection.** Perfection is a theoretical concept that does not exist in reality. You are probably waiting until the conditions are just right for it to be perfect. It will never

be right. That's cool. You only have two choices: imperfect or nothing. Stop waiting to learn one more thing, get one more opinion, or make one last tweak. Just be OK with imperfection.

14. **Pat yourself on the back.** Your need for instant gratification is probably keeping you from getting things done. You're jumping over to Facebook to see if anyone has commented on your status, or checking Twitter for an endorphin rush. You'll probably get it there. But if you have read this far, you want to get things done. Instead of turning to social media for instant gratification, tell yourself how awesome you are after you accomplish each little thing.

15. **Help someone else.** We love to help each other. It's addictive for humans. When you are working on a project and just can't seem to move forward, pick up the phone and call someone you can help. Offer some advice, feedback or expertise. This will give you a feeling of accomplishment. You'll feel good about yourself and happy that you've contributed to someone else's life. That's a much better endorphin source than social media.

There are external things you can't control.

There are always external things you can't control. From this standpoint, it's only by labeling a thought or feeling as either good or bad, productive or harmful, that you're actually getting in your own way. Restricting your creative flow.

Getting out of your own way means being with who you are, moment to moment, whether you like it or not. Whether or not it's easy or comfortable, familiar or disturbing. And then creating from that place.

When you get out of the way, you stop resisting life. The focus shifts from what you don't have to what is here and available. No longer doubting everything, you receive what life offers you.

And rather than living in the mind-created past or future, you are available to the simplicity of this now moment.

Unclouded by mental noise, you become crystal clear about what to do next. You tell the truth about what is and isn't working. And you take practical steps to begin truly living.

. . . . Get Out of Your Own Way!

Self-Discovery Challenge:

Make a list of how you are getting in your own way:

List the steps you will take to get out of your own way:

Know someone in their own way? List the name of the person below. List the steps you will take to help this person to get out of their own way:

Chapter Three

Changing Self-Talk

* * * * * * * * * * * * * * *

"Do not own your negative self-talk."
—Michele Sfakianos

Do you like yourself? This is a question I never really stopped to ask myself. I took myself for granted because I thought if everyone else liked me then I was okay. Boy was I wrong! I'm going to talk to you about Self-Esteem and Confidence. Two things I didn't lack growing up, but realized later in life, they can go by the wayside if they aren't nurtured.

Self-Esteem

Having a healthy and balanced sense of self-esteem is a major key to living a healthy and happy life. There are two sides to every coin, however. Sometimes self-esteem can become something else - namely, an unbalanced ego. So how do you know if you are simply being confident, or if you are deceiving yourself?

> "Wanting to be someone else is a waste of the person you are."
> —Marilyn Monroe

Healthy Self-Esteem: A healthy self-esteem is one where you have the confidence to be honest with yourself, and love yourself no matter what. A healthy self-esteem encourages you to live your life to the fullest, make bold but good choices, and to keep going if and when mistakes are made.

The 4-1-1 on Reinventing You . . . .

Low Self-Esteem: An unhealthy self-esteem goes two ways. On the one hand, an unhealthy self-esteem leaves you with zero confidence as well as an often unrelenting fear of making mistakes, and often leads to a poor quality of life.

Over-Inflated Self-Esteem: On the other hand, an over-inflated self-esteem is also unhealthy. This is a form of self-deception that tricks you into thinking that you are better than everyone else and that you can do anything, even to the point of ostracizing your friends and family.

An unbalanced sense of self-esteem can lower your quality of life. People with low self-esteem often miss out on some of the best things that life has to offer. Either they are too afraid to make a mistake, or they feel that they are not worthy of happiness. It's a type of existence that only holds you back.

An over-inflated sense of self-esteem puts you in danger of losing friends and close relationships. Outwardly, people with an over-inflated sense of self-esteem come off as cocky or mean. They tend to have trouble gaining and keeping close, loving relationships because they come off as being less than genuine.

Typically, however, an inflated self-esteem is generally a sign of the exact opposite. Most people like this are hiding their true selves and are actually riddled with low self-confidence. The false mask of bravado is not true self-esteem, and this confidence is really just a form of self-deception.

Understanding the Meaning of Self-Esteem

Self-esteem is defined as confidence in your own self-worth, a sense of self-respect. You are not respecting yourself if you do not believe you are worthy of respect and happiness, nor are you respecting yourself by hiding behind an inflated ego.

To truly find your own self-worth and build a true and balanced healthy self-esteem, you have to first be honest with yourself. Stop hiding behind fear or a false sense of confidence. Often, being honest with ourselves is harder than being honest with an outside person.

Self-esteem is truly a balancing act that everyone has to work on. To build a healthy and balanced self-esteem you must first and foremost be honest with yourself. Only then can you start to work on your view of the world as a whole and make real changes that could change your life for the better.

Changing Self-Talk
Confidence

"No one can make you feel inferior without your consent."
—Eleanor Roosevelt

Lack of confidence can paralyze your life. It can prevent you from doing great things just because you don't believe in yourself and can turn you into your own enemy. Lack of confidence doesn't only have a devastating effect on your mind, but is also responsible for the way other people treat you.

If you are unable to develop the self-confidence you need every aspect of your life gets affected. It affects your education, employment, relationships and social situations. However, it's never too late to recognize this and start working to improve your self-confidence to achieve what you desire in life.

> **If you are unable to develop the self-confidence you need, every aspect of your life gets affected.**

If you are able to understand the problems associated with the low level of your self-confidence, it will help you better understand the corrective steps you need to take in order to develop your self-confidence to reach higher levels. For example, if you suffer from shyness or fear it indicates a self-confidence problem. It is typical for people with low self-confidence to hide from interacting with others and avoid situations that call for such interactions. However, by making conscious efforts and using correct knowledge needed for rebuilding your self-confidence, you can gradually correct this situation.

Your mind and your emotions are the tools required for developing your self-confidence and they always remain with you. It's your mind that can eliminate negative emotions like fear and shyness and put you on a track on which you will continue for the rest of your life. First you need to see yourself in a positive light, only then will other people see you in the same way. When you have confidence in yourself, you will earn the confidence of others and command their respect. Mostly our thoughts are responsible for low self-confidence. The right way to tackle this problem is to win over negative thoughts with positive thinking. This is a sure method

The 4-1-1 on Reinventing You

for building and governing your self-confidence. Positive thinking is how you can develop yourself into a much stronger and confident individual.

Negative thoughts invariably lead to negative or even unlawful actions whereas positive thinking leads to positive actions. Your positive actions will lead to more positive thinking and result in more positive outcomes. Both positive and negative thinking are ongoing behavioral patterns. But when you are able to develop a positive mindset, you exude confidence and are well on your way to success. The key to developing your self-confidence is to start small. If you begin by doing big things to develop your self-confidence and fail, it can have a big negative outcome. So take small steps in the beginning, so that even if you fall your self-confidence isn't damaged.

Don't make the mistake of developing your self-confidence by yourself. Surround yourself with people who support you and will provide encouragement when things get tough and you start feeling low. Although it's good to have more people on your team, even if you have just one person other than you, you know you have someone who will encourage and support you.

And finally, never quit your efforts even if the results are slow in coming. Just take a firm decision that you will not quit until you develop your self-confidence to the levels you desire - no matter how tough things get or how long it takes.

Learn to Let Go and Build Back Your Confidence

Many of us are experiencing "the calm before the storm". We are under the impression that the present is just a hoax and that our life is yet to begin. We believe that all we had until today were false starts. And, when the world sees us half the way, we firmly assert that we are at the starting blocks.

The rate at which change is happening in this world, we are led to believe that change is that one sudden, spectacular and irreversible event that everyone takes note of. The need is for us to realize that, as always, change is still a gradual forward movement and involves a lot of "on" and "off" days. We give into peer pressure to make change happen and enter a vicious cycle of depression when nothing goes our way.

> **On many occasions we resist change since it can be painful and filled with a lot of uncertainties.**

Changing Self-Talk

We need to stop pondering over the bad days and failures that are few but noticeable and set our eyes on our successes that are gradual and unnoticeable immediately to the eyes. We need to "let go" of the paralyzing power of failure. That involves understanding and implementing the need to change. On many occasions we resist change since it can be painful and filled with a lot of uncertainties. We experience a false sense of security by being static and not taking risks that we know may be necessary.

If a child learning to walk decides it's better to sit than take the risk of falling down in the hallway while walking, he may never walk his entire life. Similarly, we need to look at failures as our baby steps towards the objective of building a life. Putting behind us the memories and sure signs of failure may not be easy, but must be done.

"Letting go" may require us to set short term goals, which may seem to take us in an entirely new direction. We may be apprehensive of losing sight of our goal and resist such a change. We must realize that every goal achieved, whether short or long term, is a step towards boosting our confidence and will add up to the achievement of our objectives.

Sometimes, incorporating change may make us appear as inconsistent and unsure of our goals. One example may be that of Warren Buffett, who began his business as a newspaper boy and ended up as an investment banker, all the while, unnoticed by the media or business analysts. Developing confidence doesn't have a straight and simple formula to be implemented.

One of the best examples of letting go of the worst events is that of the stock market. The analysis of the daily gains made will show a rather irregular way of growth, while the bigger picture displays a definite and prominent growth over a decade or more. Similarly, we need to look at "off" days as just a passing phenomenon compared to the long stay of slow but steady progress. In our endeavor to achieve progress let us remember progress can "bottom-out" but it has no "top-up".

Fulfilling Life

Self-confidence is one's belief in oneself. It refers to one's confidence in his actions, beliefs and competencies. Having self-confidence is the key towards a successful and fulfilling life. Self-talk can be described as that little voice inside your head which can either be beneficial or detrimental to your self-confidence. This inner voice usually critiques, give comments, or

The 4-1-1 on Reinventing You

praises one's deeds and actions. There are different views about self-talk in relation to building self-confidence. Some people may associate self-talk to the obstacles towards attaining true confidence in oneself. This can be true in the cases of people who have no drive to take the pessimism out of their heads. This can later become a vicious cycle where a person is perpetually trapped in a downward spiral of self-esteem decline.

There is also a school of thought which believes that self-talk is an important tool in developing self-confidence. The inner voice can be seen as a teacher, a mentor, or critic who gives constructive comments. Self-talk has been employed by successful people in their careers and in popular fields such as sports and show business. How do you utilize self-talk towards developing a healthy self-confidence?

Listen to your inner voice. This is the first step in making good use of self-talk. Identify the inner voice in you and listen to what it's saying. Ask questions regarding the contents of the thoughts; the situations which brought about these thoughts; and the other factors which could have aggravated the situation. Remember that this is to be done under the general goal of building self-confidence, so try to be as honest as possible.

Thoughts Assessment. After the thoughts have been identified, it's time to assess them. What are these thoughts saying in general? What attitude towards the self is being projected by these thoughts? How have I responded to these kinds of thoughts in the past? What have these kinds of thoughts instilled in me throughout the years? Have they been helpful to me and my quest towards self-confidence? The general tone of the inner voice is as important as what its saying. Negative tones should be controlled and be reversed into positive ones.

Make a difference. Dealing with your inner voice can be a daunting task. If it's hard to talk to somebody who won't listen, it's even harder to talk and listen to yourself since there can be no sensible argument that could happen.

Getting rid of the negative thoughts inside your head will give the positive thoughts some space. It's all about rephrasing the negative thoughts to make them positive. Your concept of the world is based on your views of the world. You develop self-confidence by feeling good about yourself.

. . . . Changing Self-Talk

Self-Discovery Challenge:

List at least five things you are afraid to do (not things you are afraid of i.e. spiders, but things such as speaking in public or afraid to ask someone for a referral):

Of the five things listed above, what is the worst thing that could happen if you attempt them?

List one new thing you will do this week:

The 4-1-1 on Reinventing You . . . .

List three negative thoughts (or self-talks) you currently have about yourself:

List three (or more) good qualities about yourself:

List three short-term goals you will achieve with your good qualities in the next month:

Chapter Four

Are You Up for the Challenge?

• • • • • • • • • • • • • •

"How you respond to the challenge in the second half will determine what you become after the game, whether you are a winner or a loser."
—Lou Holtz

It's already familiar to us that real progress happens when we are prone to leaving our comfort zone. And challenging yourself to do that has become something of a set rule. Wanting to believe this, we are getting in terms with it must be done. But it's not being out of your comfort zone that gives the results, it's the length of the stretch you are about to make when out of it.

And it soon becomes clear that only by challenging yourself, and making that stretch far and wide, can you achieve real success no matter what aspect of life involved.

> **Successful people always go for the next challenge, setting the bar higher than the one before.**

Successful people always go for the next challenge, setting the bar higher than the one before. Many of them realize that it's the only way to step out and make progress. And the thing that I just recently realized is that

The 4-1-1 on Reinventing You

this behavior didn't happen overnight. It's rather an act of persistence and habit. They've trained their mind to constantly set challenges, and they've become good not only at picking the next challenge, but also completing it and growing alongside it.

The truth is we all challenge ourselves from time to time. But that alone isn't enough. Even from an early age we are being taught to set a realistic goal, challenge ourselves only to the extent of staying in our comfort zone. And when realism and challenging yourself come together, we are very limited in what we can achieve.

Why is this so? Challenging yourself only within the frame of what is achievable at this moment, will never make you change; for better or for worse. What is real to you now in terms of goal setting, is only equivalent to your present capabilities. And setting your goals depending on present capabilities, means that you don't intend to change, or improve.

Therefore, your challenges must be way out there, seemingly unrealistic at the time they begin. Only then you will step out of your comfort zone in a resolute manner, reaching further than you ever have.

Did you know that it takes 30 days to form a new habit? The first few days are similar as to how you would imagine the birth of a new river. Full of enthusiasm it gushes forth, only to be met by strong obstacles. The path is not clear yet, and your surroundings don't agree. Old habits urge you to stay the same. But you need to stay determined. This starting phase is the hardest. Slowly, however, the path is cleared, resistance erodes a little day by day. And soon after, everything around you is actually helping you to go through the motions of your newfound habit. The new river is formed and flowing. By giving yourself a challenge, for a minimum of 30 days, you will find that you are able to improve all facets of your life.

So, take a moment to reflect on the question "Who do I want to be in 5 years?" What kind of habits would you like to have? You better start now if you want your new habits to influence your lifestyle and consequently your life!

You can't wait for things to be perfect before starting a project or trying to define your goals. The time will never be "just right." When it comes to your career, if you want to be an athlete, then start training. If you want to be an author, take some writing courses. Do something now – don't just wait for the perfect time.

If you want to make the most out of your career and life, you must learn to challenge yourself. You will never fulfill even a fraction of your potential

Are You Up for the Challenge?

by sticking to the safe and comfortable. The safe and comfortable never forces you to rise to the occasion or go the extra mile.

Ways to challenge yourself:
- Write down a list of your future hopes, dreams, and goals, no matter how ridiculous or crazy they seem.
- Take a course on something of interest to broaden your horizons. Learn something new to enhance your work or family life to make you more valuable.
- Set a goal every year to learn one thing new, create one new thing, and travel to a new place that you've never visited.
- Push your limits. Dare yourself to do something totally different.
- Take a moment each day to practice self-compassion and self-love.
- Expand your comfort zone. Summon the courage to step out of your comfort zone.
- Make adventures a priority. If necessary, schedule excitement into your daily schedule. This will force you to take it just as serious as other commitments, but also give you an allotted time where your focus is solely to enjoy the adventure.
- Walk/drive/run a new route to work each day.
- Meet new people. Meeting new people can bring you a new variety of adventure and excitement. When you make a new friend, they may introduce you to new interests, hobbies, music, food, and more.
- Make eye contact with five strangers throughout the day and smile like you mean it at every single one of them. The positive energy you'll receive in exchange for distributing a few extra grins to a few unsuspecting passersby will prove worthwhile.
- Pick one bad habit you have and ditch it for 30 days. If you don't miss it – never go back to it.
- Start a new hobby. Whether it's paining or collecting, a new activity is refreshing. Try collecting something rare, or bring a notebook or sketch pad wherever you go. You'll find something interesting to write down or draw.
- Practice at least one completely selfless act each day.
- Set aside an hour during which you don't respond to any of the noises your phone or other device makes to remind yourself that technology can almost always wait.
- Exercise five minutes longer than you normally do.

The 4-1-1 on Reinventing You

- Be yourself. It's hard to do this when you're trying new things, but always remember who you really are.
- Write a letter to your future self. What do you see yourself doing 5 years from now?
- Keep a journal.

Learn to always challenge yourself in different ways. The best way to always stay on your toes and stay sharp, is to challenge yourself in new and interesting fashions. New challenges keep our brains well exercised, and they inspire us to grow in new ways.

Challenging yourself does not mean over working yourself. This is indeed a challenge, but not a very creative challenge. To challenge yourself to pull on a rope is not creative, any farm horse can pull on a rope. A creative challenge would be to try and figure out how to avoid having to pull on that rope at all.

Get creative with your challenges. Learn to test yourself in different ways, challenge yourself to find better ways to do things that you have done before. Challenge yourself to become more efficient, challenge yourself to become better than before. To do this you must push yourself to think outside the box, to let go of conventions that you have lived by and to approach old problems in new ways.

By challenging yourself in different ways you will discover many things about yourself. There is no better way to discover what you are capable of and what your weaknesses are than to always and constantly do something that tests you in a different way. Life is a constant challenge but our routines tend to make us think that life is boring and simple. We are also far more complex and far stronger than we imagine, through constant challenge we can discover our great strengths and find a kind of self-confidence that would not be possible without our self-imposed tests.

Life can become far more enjoyable if we are able to constantly challenged ourselves in new and interesting ways. When things are boring, what we're really saying is that this certain situation holds no new surprises for us. This 'surprise' is what creates excitement and brings passion and fun into our lives. As Henry David Thoreau said, "most live lives of quiet desperation." This is so because we are all trapped by the weight of our routines and the lack of attention that we give to our lives. Challenge breaks routine and therefore greatly increases the amount of attention that we are paying to things. To constantly challenge yourself is the key to becoming better in all things.

Are You Up for the Challenge?

The more you challenge yourself and succeed, the greater your confidence in your ability to do it again next time. Challenge doesn't just help you grow your skills and knowledge – it helps you grow your belief that you can.

The good thing is that you will never be satisfied with mediocrity. And that alone is a huge success. It's a shift of mindset, if you will, that changes everything, the whole game in fact. Aiming to reach for more, will usually get you there.

Another thing that will radically change is your perception. Challenging yourself for more, will change the picture you have about yourself, and you will start to see yourself already there, already changed, for the better.

This will also give your self-esteem an injection similar to nothing before. Convincing yourself that you will conquer the challenge, will indeed make you believe it. And then your self-esteem and self-confidence will go through the roof.

Other people will also notice this and give you more respect since you have higher standards. That's something everyone admires. That's why I say it proud that I'm a self-improvement junkie. You and I both know what that means. We constantly challenge ourselves in everyday situations. But, it's knowing where to set the bar that will improve our capacities.

Challenging yourself in what other people would consider unrealistic, will make you stretch more, making your way to better results.

The 4-1-1 on Reinventing You

Self-Discovery Challenge

List 5 ways you want to challenge yourself:

Of the five things you listed above, list some actions items to take to achieve these:

What is one action you will take today to make a better future for yourself?

Chapter Five

Going Back to School?

• • • • • • • • • • • • • • •

"Live as if you were to die tomorrow. Learn as if you were to live forever."
—Mahatma Gandhi

Going back to college at 40+ years can feel intimidating for a lot of reasons. When you have other financial responsibilities, like a mortgage and family expenses, finding thousands of dollars for tuition can be challenging. Then of course there's the aspect of readjusting to being a student after many years out of school...not to mention the apprehension that can come along with learning new technologies, or the thought of enrolling in classes with people half your age.

> **Making the decision whether or not to go back to school is a highly personal one, and it should take you some time to think through it.**

Yes, it's overwhelming, but it doesn't mean you can't or shouldn't do it. Making the decision whether or not to go back to school is a highly personal one, and it should take you some time think through it.

If you are thinking of returning to school to pick up new skills for your journey, investigate the likely pay (and availability) of the career you're

The 4-1-1 on Reinventing You

aiming for. If you want to start your own business, make sure to search salaries for that type of business in your area. Your education will be worth the cost only if you'll earn more, after tax, than you paid for the course – including the interest you will pay on educational loans.

When you borrow, there are two rules of thumb:
1. The total amount of your loan, for all school years, should not exceed the first-year salary you expect from your new job or business.
2. You should be able to repay that loan, in full, within 10 years. Don't go into retirement carrying a student loan.

Do you need a degree? Think about how much education you'll actually need. Four-year degree programs are expensive and might not pay off for people starting late in life. Perhaps you can fulfill your ambitions in two years with an associate degree. Or consider just taking the courses you need and forego the degree. Your best choice might be a public community college. These schools offer a wide variety of vocational programs at modest cost.

Beware of the expensive for-profit schools that advertise aggressively. Often they provide inferior or inappropriate training. Search online for complaints about any school you're considering.

Would a certification in a specific field be a better choice for you? There are many certifications for different areas of interest and the cost is much lower (most times) for the certification versus a degree. Make sure to compare tuition with certification cost. Include fees, books and other associated costs in the comparison.

Looking for free money? There are education grants available for people pursuing certain fields. Put the words "grants for [your specialty]" into a search engine and see what turns up. If you're currently working, your employer might offer tuition money to help improve your skills.

Speaking of free money – complete a FAFSA form (Free Application for Federal Student Aid, available at fafsa.ed.gov) to see if you're eligible for aid based on financial need. People who never received a bachelor's degree might get a federal Pell Grant, which is only for undergraduates. Some states provide tuition waivers for older students or people who are unemployed.

If you need to borrow money for higher education, and you aren't eligible for the FAFSA, you can get an unsubsidized loan at a fixed interest rate.

You can also turn to private lenders, but remember to borrow no more than you expect to earn in your first year (second year for self-employment). And – don't use your high interest credit cards to finance your education!

If the thought of physically going to classes doesn't interest you, consider earning a degree online. Many reputable schools offer distance education via the internet for cable TV. By staying in state, you get more favorable tuition rates. Again, though, beware of those schools that advertise heavily and make sure to search for complaints online.

When making a budget, consider all of the costs – not just tuition but also commuting, books, laptops, babysitters, and expensive supplies that might be needed in class. You might need to purchase additional equipment for the course, so make sure you know all of this up front.

Whatever you choose, be sure you have the time and motivation to do the classwork. You'll need to complete the program to compete in your area of expertise.

Make a plan

Using your goals and pain points, make a plan to determine if going back to school is the right option for you. Include all of the costs and other practicalities that would impact your choice.

Here are some points to consider:
- Day-to-day logistics of your personal life. If you have children, factor in their schedules. Include your personal schedule too, like working out, cooking meals, household chores and similar details.
- Scheduling options. Keep in mind that you don't have to attend school full-time. You can enroll part-time or take online classes.
- Take advantage of helpful resources. Universities have resources available to help you with your decision-making process. While making your plan, consult with people who can help answer your questions.
- Learn what the classes will be like. If you plan on taking online courses, research what the virtual classroom environment will be like and what equipment you'll need to participate. If you plan on attending on campus, try observing a class or visiting the campus for a tour.

College is no longer a young person's domain. Older Americans are heading back to school, not because it's expected of them to keep up with

The 4-1-1 on Reinventing You

the younger generation, but because they want to. Fortunately for them, online and hybrid programs are making it easy to schedule study times around work and family events, and many returning students are taking full advantage of these flexible education options.

Don't let age hold you back from attending college. Create your goal, figure out your pain points and make a plan. You might just discover that going back to school over the age of 40 is the best decision you ever made!

. . . . Going Back to School?

Self-Discovery Challenge:

Will you obtain a degree or certification, or just take courses of interest?

List the schools you are thinking about attending:

Once you have narrowed down the selections, make a list of the expenses required:

The 4-1-1 on Reinventing You

What sacrifices will you make to be able to return to school?

How will you schedule time to study?

After going through this exercise, is there anything still holding you back? If so, what? What will you do to overcome this hurdle?

Chapter Six

Who's Your Mentor?

*"Tell me and I forget, teach me and I may remember,
involve me and I learn."*
—Benjamin Franklin

To be successful you must be willing to take risks. One of the risks that can generate the greatest fear is the word no. There are other reasons that people are afraid to ask others for help, such as looking foolish, stupid, or too needy. No one wants to feel rejected and the word no is the biggest rejection of all.

> **To be successful you must be willing to take risks.**

Many successful individuals have asked other people for help at some time in their career. They didn't consider asking as a sign of weakness, neither should you. Asking is a sign that you want to grow. It shows that you will do what it takes for your own success. If you don't ask questions to get what you want, aren't you already telling yourself "no" in advance?

So just how do you ask someone for help? You want to ask as if you expect to get what you want.

When you plan your goals, you will want to look at other successful people and model after what they did to achieve their success. You will want to seek out a good mentor to help you along the way.

Before you decide you need a mentor, you should fully understand your situation.

The 4-1-1 on Reinventing You

- You need to determine why you are stuck and what your struggles are. Identify your pain points.
- Make a list of exactly what you need help with. Do you need assistance with marketing, coaching on personal objectives?
- You will want to think about people close to you that you could ask for help. This could be your colleagues, family members or friends. Have they offered you help in the past?
- Match people with tasks based on their interests, strengths, time needed and your comfort level with them.
- You should then determine how you would ask for help.
- Make the decision to ask.

There are three types of mentors:

1. **Direct**. Someone who is in front of you who will show you how they did it.

2. **Indirect**. Books. You can outsource 50 percent of mentorship to books and other materials. However, 150-500 books equal one good mentor. If you have time to read, it's a great help. People ask me, "What is a good book to read?" The types of books would be: inspirational, self-help, personal growth and leadership. Whatever your beliefs, underline them through reading every day.

3. **Everything is a mentor**. If you are at zero, and have passion for reinvention, then everything you look at will be a metaphor for what you want to do. The tree you see, with roots you don't, with underground water that feeds it, is a metaphor for personal growth if you connect the dots. And everything you look at, you will connect the dots.

What can a mentor do for you?
- Mentors can help you navigate the road more smoothly. You can benefit from their wisdom and experience. A good mentor will get to know you, and can speak into your life with the benefit of their past experiences.
- Mentors bring a fresh perspective. They can help you understand yourself better and see things as they are.
- A good mentor will make you ask the hard questions. They will help

you consider what you need and where you want to go. If you don't know this beforehand, you haven't thought about it enough. **Mentors aren't there to make your decisions for you**. Mentors make you think.
- Mentors will reassure you about your struggles. They may have had the very same struggles earlier in their life.

Here are ten steps to finding that person:
1. **Look at the people you know.** Look around at the people in your personal and professional life. Is there someone you admire? Someone you would like to emulate in some way? Someone who has the wisdom you need?

2. **Consider people you've never met.** Research the top individuals in the businesses, organizations and associations of your chosen field. Find out as much as you can about them. Identify those individuals whose values and accomplishments you most admire.

3. **Select a mentor who is a good role model.** Look for someone who is not only famous or successful, but who has a reputation for character and solid principles. Look for someone you can admire and respect as well as emulate.

4. **Select a mentor who is a good listener.** The best mentor is one who gets to know you – your skills and strengths and weaknesses, your individual personality and your aspirations. A good mentor should not serve as a lecturer, but as a sounding board who will help you with your struggles and help you to clarify your principles and beliefs.

5. **Select a mentor who levels with you.** A good mentor doesn't just encourage you, but will also tell you the blunt truth when you are moving in the wrong direction. It is also a good sign if your mentor is candid and open about his or her own life. Anyone who has accomplished great things has made mistakes along the way and will share those experiences freely so that you can learn from them.

6. **Look for someone who is unlike you in some important way.** Our tendency is to gravitate toward those with whom we have a lot in

The 4-1-1 on Reinventing You

common. But in seeking out a mentor, it is wise to seek out people who have strengths that we lack. For example, if you are a shy and introverted person, seek out someone who is bold and out-going. Instead of pairing up with someone who will reinforce your weaknesses, find someone who will challenge you to acquire new strengths.

7. **Be open to finding a mentor in unlikely places.** We tend to think of a mentor or teacher as someone with gray hair and a well-lined face. Not necessarily! A mentor could be anyone who has something to teach you and could be the same age or even younger than you. A mentor could be someone of lower rank and social standing than you.

8. **If the person doesn't know you, approach that person with a brief letter of introduction.** You might say, "I have followed your achievements in the field of _____ and I eagerly read your book on _____. Like you, I am very concerned about the issue of _____ and I hope to make a contribution in these areas myself someday. I am looking for a mentoring relationship, and I would be grateful if you could spare thirty minutes to discuss such a possibility with me."

9. **Make personal contact. Don't be shy.** Ask, "Would you be willing to mentor me?" You may think you are imposing on that person, but I have found that most people who have achieved a place of accomplishment in life are eager to share their wisdom, experience, and knowledge with others. When you ask someone to be your mentor, you are truly offering them high praise.

10. **Remember, you are never too old to be mentored.** I have reached a point where I know I have a lot of knowledge and experience to offer others – but I still have a lot to learn! That's why, despite my age, I still seek out people to mentor me.

Once you know the issues you struggle with and the person you would like to ask for help from, ask in this way:
- Be polite. Remember you are asking for a person's time and knowledge.

- Start by telling them why you want their help. Your prospective mentor wants to know why you chose them and not someone else. Tell them what you think their strengths are and why they are a good fit.
- Be specific on what you need help with, what form you want that help to take, and how you envision the end result of your meetings. Make a specific request so they know what they are agreeing to.
- Be clear that you will suit their schedule – not yours. What type of meetings will you have? Will the meetings be through the computer (Skype or other software), by phone, or in person? Allow them to determine the meeting type, time and place for the meetings, and for how long the meeting will last.
- Accommodate – after all they are helping you.

Don't feel that you are placing a burden on someone if you ask them for help. If someone asks you for help, do you feel they are a burden? I think you would feel good to know that someone respects you enough to ask.

When mentors give you advice, follow it. No one likes to waste their time. You need to at least try the ideas and strategies and see if they will work for you. Try doing what they do and reading what they have read. If these new ways of thinking and actions work, adopt them and make them your habits. If not, discard them and keep looking for new and better ways. Don't continue to utilize techniques that will not benefit you.

You want to allow yourself to feel worthy of being helped by others. Think about all of the times when people were of help to you and you didn't even ask. Use those memories as a starting point to change your self-sabotaging thinking and behaviors.

If you ask someone for help and they say no what is the worst that can happen? The answer: Nothing. You just need to move on to another person to ask. You never have anything to lose by asking, and because there's everything to gain, you need to ask.

Remember, the first time you do anything is the hardest. After that first time, asking will come more natural and you will get the results you want.

The 4-1-1 on Reinventing You

Self-Discovery Challenge

List 3 things you have wanted to ask for help with, but haven't yet.

Of the 3 things you listed above, list how and why you are stopping yourself from asking for help.

How would your life be better if you ask? How much faster would you reach your goals?

. . . . Who's Your Mentor?

Of the 3 listed in #1, pick one issue and write the name of the person you are going to ask for help from:

Pick someone to mentor. Select a person to help grow: a coworker or employee, your child, a fellow church member, etc. Write the name of that person below and when you will start:

Chapter Seven

Take Time to Declutter

*"Clutter can distract you, weigh you down, and in general,
it invites chaos into your life."*
—Michele Sfakianos

There was a time, several years ago, when my life was cluttered. I had too much stuff, and it kept coming in all the time. I had too much to do, and didn't know how to simplify my schedule.
I was in need of some decluttering, and I knew it.

> **Combined, small steps will lead to big improvements that will be easier to maintain over the long run.**

Excessive clutter is often a symptom and a cause of stress and can affect every facet of your life, from the time it takes you to do things, to your finances, and your overall enjoyment of life. Clutter can distract you, weigh you down, and in general it invites chaos into your life. Oftentimes, however, tackling the clutter can seem an insurmountable task if you don't know where or how to start. By devoting a little of your time to getting rid of the clutter in your life and maintaining things relatively clutter-free, you'll reap the rewards of pleasing living areas, reduced stress, and a more organized and productive existence.

The 4-1-1 on Reinventing You

The best way to tackle the decluttering of your home, your work space, and your life is to take things one small step at a time. Combined, small steps will lead to big improvements that will be easier to maintain over the long run.

When I started to change my habits, from being stationary to exercising, to being more mindful, simplifying my life was near the top of the list.

The question became, how to go about it? How do you start when you're facing a mountain of clutter, and another mountain of commitments, and piles of files and mail and email and other digital information?

Answer: Keep it simple as you go. Simple, each step of the way. That said, I found complications that made things harder at every turn.

Declutter Your Physical Environment

This applies to the physical space you spend your time in on a day-to-day basis: your home, workspace and even your car. Aside from getting rid of the things you don't use anymore, you should also eliminate the items that are not invited into the next phase of your life with you.

Picture the vision you hold for yourself — the abundance you want, the success you need to achieve, and the place you want to be by the end of the year. Is that old stained T-shirt or towel with holes welcome in that picture?

Go through every room in the house, every drawer and cabinet. Evaluate if what you're finding meets the high standard of the improved version of your life you're working toward. How many spices in your cabinet have never been used? Are you ever going to find the lid for that Tupperware? How about socks without matches or clothes that don't fit? They don't belong here, I promise.

When you physically remove these things, you create space for new, improved items. Recently I spent a lot of time decluttering my bathroom of old makeup and half-used lotions or soaps, and the next day a gift from a friend showed up on my door step full of chemical-free, mostly organic self-care goodies. Clear that space so the abundance can come in.

To get started:
- Take just 10 minutes today to sort through a pile, or declutter a shelf or table or countertop. Put everything into one pile, and start with the first thing you pick up (no putting things back in the pile). Keep a "donation" box handy.

Take Time to Declutter

- Ask yourself: Do you really need this? Do you use it regularly? Do you love it? If the answer to any of these is no, then recycle, donate, or give it to someone who might want it. Put it in the box for these purposes.
- Put things back that you need/use/love, with space between things. This is their "home" and you should always put them back there.
- Stop after 10 minutes, continue tomorrow for another 10 minutes, and so on, one small spot in your home at a time.
- If you want to do more than 10 minutes, go ahead, but be careful not to overdo it in the beginning or you'll think it's difficult and not want to continue.

Keep Going: Once you've gotten the ball rolling, here's how to keep going:
- Keep decluttering in small bits. Pick an area to focus on each week.
- Don't worry about perfection. Do it a little at a time. You can always declutter it more later.
- Put your box of donation/recycling/giving away in your trunk to get rid of next time you're out. Email friends/family to ask if they want things — often you can find a good home for perfectly good things you don't really use (like that workout equipment).
- If you're on the fence, use a Maybe Box (put things that you think you might need in a box, mark it with today's date, put a reminder on your calendar 6 months from now to check on the Maybe Box. If you haven't used it in 6 months, you probably don't need it and can get rid of it.
- Get help. Sometimes you just can't bear to part with your stuff, but if you can get an outside person to help make the decision (friend or family member), they can help you to talk through the need or use of the item.
- Enjoy the space. Once you've decluttered an area, really focus on how much you love the simplified space. Once you're hooked on this simplicity, you're more likely to keep going.

Decluttering Your Calendar & Digital Life

Physical decluttering is only one type of decluttering. You can also simplify your day, and your online/computer life as well.
- Decluttering your day is about reducing commitments, and saying no to the non-essential things. So first make a list of your

The 4-1-1 on Reinventing You

commitments. Many times our lives are too cluttered with all of the things that we need to do at home, work, school, in our religious or civic lives, with friends and family, with hobbies, and so on. Take a look at each area of your life and write down all of your commitments. Seeing it all written down can be quite an eye-opening experience, as well as overwhelming. From here, look at each one and decide whether it really brings you joy and value, and if it's worth the amount of time that you invest in it. Another way to reduce your commitments is to identify a few that you truly love, and get rid of the rest. Learn how to say no and decline offers. If you eliminate the things that don't bring you joy or value, you'll have more time for the things that you love.

- Make a list of what's most important to you (4-5 things) and declutter the rest. Say no to people with a phone call or email, and get out of existing commitments.
- Be very ruthless about saying no to new commitments — and seeing requests as potential commitments. Guard your time.
- Declutter your computer. Get rid of files and programs on your computer that you don't need. Get rid of most or all of the icons on your desktop. They not only slow down your computer, but they also create visual clutter. There are better ways of accessing your information. Regularly purge old, unused files. If organization is not your thing, utilize a program such as Google Desktop to search for your files when you need them.
- Declutter information. In the digital world of today, there are so many different ways that information creeps into our lives. Information in itself can become overwhelming when you have too much of it, and this is called information clutter. Instead of letting information take over your life, set limits. Reduce the number of things that you read each day and get rid of things from your RSS feeds. Chuck those magazine subscriptions, and reduce your consumption of news and television. I'm not suggesting that you cut yourself off from the world, just setting some boundaries will help. Instead of letting information, even the kind that friends share on Facebook, take over your life, control how and when you receive it by limiting what you read.

. . . . **Take Time to Declutter**

Declutter your digital life one step at a time, just like your physical life. Email newsletters, blogs, social networks, online reading and watching, forums, etc.—are they essential? Can you declutter them?

Dealing with Others

Having other people in your life (home or workspace) can make simplifying more complicated.

- Talk to them about it early on, when you're just thinking about it. Don't force a decision on anyone, but involve them in the decision-making process.
- Focus on the benefits, the why, rather than what they need to do and why what they're doing is wrong. People don't like to be wrong, but they do like benefits.
- Lead by example. Show how you can declutter your space, and how much nicer it is, and how much easier it is to find things, to clean, to be at peace during your day.
- If there's resistance, focus on decluttering your space. Don't get frustrated with them, because that makes it more difficult. Instead, remember that you were a clutter-holic not long ago, so empathize.
- Don't shy away from an opportunity to discuss simplifying, and why you're doing it, in a positive way. Criticizing doesn't help, nor does acting superior. Instead - inspire.

When I suggest to others that they need to declutter their homes and relationships to achieve the success they want in their life, I'm typically met with some skepticism. If you've never thought about it before, it can be confusing to think that the things we keep with us physically and mentally can have an impact on our business lives.

In truth, however, clutter in our physical environments and relationships energetically blocks the flow of abundance, getting in the way of the success we are reaching for.

> **When we have clutter and unwanted stuff in our lives, there isn't space for the abundance we are seeking.**

The 4-1-1 on Reinventing You . . . .

But it makes sense, doesn't it? When we have clutter and unwanted stuff in our lives, there isn't space for the abundance we are seeking. We want more money, nicer clothes, more delicious food, yet all we have is lots of mediocre, old, unused crap taking up our precious space.

This applies to our mental and emotional environments as well. Often we hold onto resentment and deny forgiveness, then wonder why it's so challenging to feel grateful and truly appreciate the things we have that matter.

If you're serious about manifesting and welcoming abundance into your life, here are some ways you can declutter relationships and emotional baggage.

Declutter Your Relationships

It might feel a little unnatural to talk about decluttering your relationships like you would do with your belongings, but similar rules apply. We're all directly influenced by the people we choose to surround ourselves with; that's something we learn at school and carry with us through the rest of our lives. To declutter your relationships, you need to be around people who love and support you. When you're looking to attract abundance, surrounding yourself with others who are abundant is extremely important.

Declutter Your Emotional Baggage

Practice forgiveness — forgiving yourself and others.

- Get rid of the fear that lives in your head. This fear will confuse you, keep you playing small, and get in the way of your success.
- Stop procrastinating and prioritize. Delegate and eliminate all of it so you aren't drowning in overwhelming feelings.
- Allow yourself to see past the things that have hurt or disappointed you and visualize them as stepping stones and lessons to be learned from.
- Release your frustration. This is a must if you want live in the present and not the past.

> **Everyone has emotional clutter.**

Everyone has emotional clutter. It's natural. The important thing is to recognize and declutter your emotional baggage so that it doesn't prevent

Take Time to Declutter

you from seeing and taking the opportunities that are right in front of us. When you can release the painful baggage you've been hanging onto, great transformation is possible.

Once you've successfully decluttered, whether it be one area or all the areas mentioned above, clutter will inevitably begin to creep back into your life. You must be vigilant in weeding it out on a regular basis, or it will just take over your life again.

- Set up a system to keep clutter in check. Examine the way that you do things and how things make their way into your life, and consider whether you can put together a simple system for everything, from your laundry, to work projects, and email. Write down your system step-by-step and try to follow them as best as you can. Follow your systems and you'll keep the clutter minimized.
- Don't slack off. It's easy to put things off for another day, but it'll save you headaches in the long run if you deal with things immediately. Throw it out, donate it, or keep it, and put it in a designated area.

There's no reason to be surrounded by things that don't work, that you don't need, or that you don't even like. Being organized isn't about getting rid of everything you own or trying to become a different person; it's about living the way you want to live, but better. There are enough things in the world that you can't control—but you can bring some order into your home and your life.

The 4-1-1 on Reinventing You . . . .

Self-Discovery Challenge:

In what areas of your life, do you need to declutter? (Schedule, friends, home, closet, etc.)

What room in your home will you start with? (Name, Date/Time to start and end)

Do you have emotional baggage? If so, what is the first step you will take to rid yourself of this baggage?

Chapter Eight

Be Grateful

• • • • • • • • • • • • • • • • •

"Be grateful for whoever comes, because each has been sent as a guide from beyond."
—Rumi

Did you know that gratitude is the very first step to receiving and actually experiencing what you desire? Gratefulness means you are real, genuine, and are remarkably positive that you have already received the very thing or situation or outcome that is yet to come. You have faith, along with a loving, kind demeanor. You truly expect to receive good things. You have no doubt.

> **Being grateful is a daily practice allowing yourself to be present in the "Now."**

Being grateful is a daily practice allowing yourself to be present in the "Now." It becomes a way of living, day in and day out. It is not a magic lamp that is pulled out in times of need, rubbed, then put back away again to be used later. You have to be genuine. The great news is that people who practice living this way live happier lives filled with abundance. Here are 5 new ways to look at this new attitude:

1. **Right Here, Right Now.** Forget multi-tasking. Be in this moment. Be fully present. Do one thing at a time. Be okay with not doing

The 4-1-1 on Reinventing You

anything. Thinking is highly over-rated. Most people are so busy thinking about what is or is not happening, or how much more they have to do, that they don't look around and notice what's happening right now. There is no past, no future moment. There is only this moment. Right here, right now. We are either happy and embrace this moment, or we are unhappy and wanting for this moment to pass so the next moment can arrive.

2. **Have an Attitude of Gratitude.** Stop comparing your life to everyone else's. There is only one you and therefore any "standard" of comparison is irrelevant, arbitrary and completely unscientific. The only comparison that makes sense is are we doing better than we did yesterday? The only person we can change is ourselves. By changing ourselves, we become a better person. Silently, we lead by example. When asked for advice, we don't offer it. Instead, we share our experience. Anyone can argue with an opinion, but no one can argue with what your personal experience has been. Besides, sharing your experience is sharing wisdom. You are not telling them they must do what you have done, but allowing them to draw their own conclusions. If they are wise, they will see to get what you have, they must do what you've done. Whatever the mind focuses on, magnifies. With an "Attitude of Gratitude" as our framework, it's easy to keep our focus on our own improvement.

3. **The Law of Attraction.** The Law of Attraction is often misunderstood and therefore some people get results while others become disillusioned by the notion that it's possible. Let's start by looking at the definition. The law of attraction is the name given to the maxim "like attracts like" which is used to sum up the idea that by focusing on positive or negative thoughts a person brings positive or negative experiences into their life. The idea being that thoughts either positive or negative have energy, one can use their thoughts to make things happen. Good things are always happening to people who are grateful. Being grateful is synonymous with love and positivity. This higher vibration attracts and returns things that are also of this same vibration.

Be Grateful

You're happy, living in the now, things are good, you're putting out this energy, and remarkable things of the same high vibration are jetting their way towards you right this moment. Gratitude attracts more of that which you are grateful for and deeply desire. Be grateful for all that you have and know that all your needs are already taken care of by your Higher Power. Gratitude attracts exactly what you desire and allows you to receive it quickly. The trick is to be very specific and to know what and how to say it.

4. **Be in Love with Now.** The special key to learning to accept everything that you already have (good or not so great) is to love the present moment – all of it – and you're okay with that. You turn over everything you can't control to the Universe. All things you can do, you get busy and get those things done. You drop resentments and forgive freely, even if the other person harmed you first. This will put you in a place where you feel calm and relaxed, which is the state for seeing, hearing and experiencing life's most precious gifts – a deep connection to "All That Is". This is a high, spiritual vibration. Children sense it and will be attracted to you. Strangers will respond to you as you say "hello" or "good morning" unexpectedly to them.

5. **Letting Go.** Just how does one develop gratitude? It's already inside of you. It's not something you need to go out and get. Rather, it's something you have instant access to by connecting to all that is within in you. Gratitude is love. The attitude part simply means a way of living. The attitude of gratitude is a way of living a loving life. Being kind and loving to all. Being grateful means letting go of all resistance. Gratitude allows you to understand you at a deeper spiritual level so you have a deeper understanding about the path to come. It doesn't mean that you know everything, but it does heighten your confidence level that everything is going to turn out okay and that you can relax, knowing that you've turned everything you can't control over to your Higher Power or the Universe and that with Him, all things are possible.

It is us that are the ones that limit life and our own potential.

The 4-1-1 on Reinventing You

I found the song lyrics below that are a great expression of gratitude:

Attitude of Gratitude by David Woodward

Been thinking a lot about gratitude
Seems to me that it's a whole lot more than attitude
More than just saying thanks it's the things you do
It's what you cherish
What you hold dear to you
Been thinking a whole lot about attitude
The way you face the world the way it faces you
When you give back the good it gives to you
You only get more
You never lose
I got the feeling
I want to say thanks
For all the love and the healing
And all the beautiful things
The gratitude I'm feeling
Has got me wanting to sing
My thanks to the world
And all the good that it brings
We've all had troubles and we've felt some pain
There are times when things don't go my way
But in the end I can look and say
See all the good things that we have today
Attitude of gratitude
It's in a feeling,
in a mood,
it's in the way you move
Thank you
It makes you feel you want to give
and give the more you get
Attitude of gratitude
When you recognize
the sacrifice
It builds a deep respect
Thank you

Be Grateful

Self-Discovery Challenge:

The Gratitude Challenge involves three basic steps:

1) Think of someone who has done something important and wonderful for you, yet who has not been properly thanked.

2) Reflect on the benefits you received from this person, and write a letter expressing your gratitude for all he or she has done for you. Tell them why you are grateful for them; don't be afraid to say what is in your heart.

3) Arrange to deliver the letter personally, and spend some time with this person talking about what you wrote. If you are unable to deliver in person, mail or email your letter and express the desire to have delivered in person.

The 4-1-1 on Reinventing You

Each day when you awaken, and every night before you go to sleep, list 5 things, people or qualities you are grateful for. Keep a journal next your bed to record these items.

Chapter Nine

Step Out in Faith

• • • • • • • • • • • • • • •

"I believe in Christianity as I believe that the sun has risen: not only because I see it, but because by it I see everything else."
—C.S. Lewis

Your dream is one of the most effective cures for fear. It can fuel the flames of desire within you until you're willing to confront and overcome your fear. Your dream can help you go where you're afraid to go and do what you're afraid to do.

Fear = False Evidence Appearing Real.

> **Your dream is the most effective cure for fear.**

Most us probably fear things that we shouldn't really fear—like a routine dentist appointment or that teeny tiny crawling spider—and even though we realize, rationally, that we shouldn't fear something so silly, we just can't seem to help it. Most of the time these little fears don't hinder us too much, but there are times when they can prevent us from making positive choices—like going to the dentist every six months—and there are times when they can prevent us from living in the present—like when you spend time outside searching for potential bug encounters.

Are you frustrated because you know you're not doing what you are meant to do? Are you letting fear rule you? Learning to fight with faith is the answer.

The 4-1-1 on Reinventing You . . . .

I wonder how many people actually have gifts and talents from God but they aren't using them because they tried once and failed?

So many people are frustrated because they know they're not doing what they are meant to do and are letting fear rule them.

I want you to get a revelation about this because you're not going to ever be really happy if you don't fulfill your potential and be who God created you to be. The key is to learn who you are in Christ and see yourself in Him.

So whatever Jesus is, we are too. He is strong, and in Him, we are strong. He is courageous; in Him, we are courageous. He is a conqueror, so we can be too. He has peace and joy, so we have peace and joy. He's capable and bold. In Christ, we can do whatever we need to do with His boldness.

Everyone experiences fear in their life. There are big fears we are very aware of and little ones we may not even realize we have.

I've learned that it's very important to understand what fear is and how it works against us because if we don't, it can keep us from becoming what God created us to be, which means we won't fulfill our purpose in life.

Mind-crippling, spine-tingling, heart-stomping fear – we've all experienced it at one time or another. We're not talking about the good kind of fear that alerts your spirit to an approaching enemy, that moves you into action to protect the ones you love, or that promotes a healthy respect for God. Those fears are healthy. And not all fears are irrational. Some move in and out quickly without disrupting our lives.

But what about the other kind? Where does irrational fear originate? And how do you keep those fears from taking permanent residence in your life?

The problem with such thoughts is that they bring with them unwarranted anxiety and stress. If you would rather not experience the emotional fallout due to irrationality, here are 10 ways to arrest this kind of thinking.

1. **Address your emotional responses**. The first key to dealing with any fear is admitting to it (not always easy if, say, the fear is a bug and you are an adult!). And the next key thing is to recognize your emotional (and physical—heart beating fast, muscles tensing up, palms sweating) responses to the fear. Sometimes fear—especially the irrational kind—can take over and we don't even realize how afraid we are of something until we start paying attention to our own signals. When we pay attention to how we are feeling and

when we are feeling that way, we are able to work with those emotional responses rather than simply react to them.

2. **Consider negativity as a red flag.** Irrationality is often characterized by negativity. Perhaps the idea came from your own insecurity or it could have been an insinuation from another person that you somehow internalized. But whenever you put forth an idea that somehow brings you down, STOP. Take a step back. Ask yourself: What is the basis of this idea that I have? Am I being paranoid? Am I blowing this incident way out of proportion? Am I being inflexible? More importantly, if I continue with this line of thought, is it in any way conducive to personal growth? Am I not hurting myself with this kind of thinking?

3. **Turn negativity into affirmation.** Decide not to passively accept defeat and irrational thinking. Ask yourself: "So what? Even if it were true, does it necessarily mean that I am powerless to change it?" Restructure your thinking in such a way as to encourage positive change: "I will rise above this. I will not put myself down. I believe I am a good person and I deserve to be happy."

4. **Meditate and be mindful of your strengths and weaknesses.** Meditation is one way of keeping yourself grounded, and keeping your thoughts in line. It can be partly introspection, partly therapy. You can discipline your mind to be calm as you sort out these thoughts, removing the ideas that cause the worst damage. Face your fears from a safe headspace.

5. **Ask for advice.** You are not alone. Do not be embarrassed to ask for advice. You may also compare your version of reality with that of other people, particularly those people close to you whom you can count on to tell you the truth. This is not about letting other people think for you – it's about looking at all sides of the equation. So you have a theory. Test your theory. Gather more data. Compare or contrast. Alter your version so that it encompasses more than just your narrow viewpoint. This is also a way of gaining perspective.

6. **Use your senses to stay present.** While I'm anticipating the worse, I'm missing out on what's actually happening in the present—what I can see, smell, taste, touch, and hear. Instead of directing my attention to what I'm going to be afraid of it in the future, it's best for me to focus on what's happening now, which includes all of the beautiful things around me. Rather than worry about what's coming, we need to redirect our attention to what's here.

7. **Get (gradual) exposure to what you fear.** It can be hard to actually expose yourself to what you're afraid of (just looking at photos of spiders online sends shivers of disgust down my spine), but when the fear must be conquered, it's key to start gradually coming to terms with the fear. I've started doing this by looking at them online, and, while I won't say it's really helped that much yet, I have a feeling I'll be less surprised when I encounter one of these guys in real life.

8. **Recall what you've conquered.** I've been through many different fearful circumstances in my life and each and every time I've made it through; I've conquered this same scenario many times. Even when I recall the unpleasant experiences I've had, I realize that, in the big picture, most things don't really impact my life that much. The irrational fear is just that—irrational—and by revisiting the situations you've already been through, you will feel stronger and more ready to take on your fear.

9. **Take it one day at a time.** This might seem like a cliché saying, but it has a lot of merit, especially when it comes to coping with fear. Instead of worrying about the unpleasant things coming, focus on today. The unpleasantry hasn't arrived. And when it does, focus on that day and that moment instead of worrying about whether or not your fear will take over. To cope with any irrational fear, it can be so helpful to take it one day, hour, or minute at a time. Instead of worrying about the future—the trick is to focus on getting through little bits of time. It's much easier to master a fear when you tell yourself you only have to do it for a short period of time. And all those short periods of time add up.

10. **Be kind to yourself.** You are not the first person to think or behave irrationally. You will not be the last. People do it all the time. The point is not that you have irrational thoughts but what you do to minimize their impact on you. Maybe, just maybe, your overthinking is just a signal to take better care of yourself. Are you eating or sleeping right? Manage your habits. Are you stressed at work and haven't had a vacation in a while? Go on leave and pamper yourself a little. You do not have to be strong all of the time. You do not always have to have your ducks in a row. Give yourself a break.

Recognize that irrational fear does not originate with God. *For God has not given us a spirit of fear, but of power and of love and of a sound mind* (1 Timothy 1:7).

> **Fear is a tool the devil uses against us to make us miserable and destroy our lives.**

Fear is a tool the devil uses against us to make us miserable and destroy our lives. It begins as a thought and then creates emotions that can rule us. It often becomes a strong, intense feeling that tries to move us to make a foolish action or tries to prevent us from doing something that would be good for us. Because it's such a common way that Satan attacks people's lives, I think of it as the master spirit he uses to manipulate people and keep them out of God's will.

Simply put, fear is the opposite of faith. God wants us to walk by faith, and Satan wants us to walk by fear. When we learn to live by faith and not let fear rule our life, we can live a fulfilling, satisfying, peaceful and joyful life.

Listen to these words and adapt them as your own:

As I begin each new day, I step out in faith. I am excited to know that God has given me all I need to have a great life. The energy, life, and love of Spirit move through me easily and effortlessly. I open to divine ideas and discern what is mine to do. I am blessed with unlimited possibilities to experience life. I feel one with all that is. I feel certain that my circumstances will work out favorably, perhaps in unimaginable ways. I am meant to live a great life!

The 4-1-1 on Reinventing You

Self-Discovery Challenge:
List your strongest fears. (Public speaking, pests, heights, etc.)

What fear stands in the way of your next step on your journey?

· **Step Out in Faith**

List steps you will take to overcome this fear.

Is there someone you can ask for advice in tackling your fear? List the name of the person and the date/time you will ask for advice.

The 4-1-1 on Reinventing You

What is something you will do this week to be kind to yourself?

Chapter Ten

Creating Goals

"With ordinary talent and extraordinary perseverance, all things are attainable."
—Thomas Fowell Buxton

The alarm rings, you wake up. You turn off the alarm and start the series of rituals that would get you showered, dressed, fed with breakfast, and eventually on your way to work. You kiss your spouse on the cheek. You say your goodbyes.

> "With ordinary talent and extraordinary perseverance, all things are attainable."
> —Thomas Fowell Buxton

As you take your car from the driveway, you notice that all is quiet in the early dawn. You like to leave for work early to get away from the traffic. The trip is uneventful and the radio blares out music you have no fondness for. As you arrive at work, you check your mail/email, and start work with a cup of coffee. Lunch comes and goes. You think about saving enough to run a small business in a few years. You have told yourself the same thing for three years now.

What's wrong with this picture? Is this you? Does the same dreary day pass by, one after the other, and you suddenly realize you're forty-five and

The 4-1-1 on Reinventing You

feel you have little time left? Don't let this happen. Start setting goals with a timeline. Set goals by the SMART method.

The SMART method of setting goals has been around for a long time and has been used by many people. It's one of the many tools used by executives to hit their goals realistically and consistently with enough room to adjust to unforeseen circumstances. Setting goals is a mind game that needs to be revisited as often as possible. This is to establish the goal consistently in the mind of the goal setter. Eventually the goal setter will have no need to be reminded of the goals he sets for himself.

SMART is an acronym for the following bywords:

Specific – The goal has to be as detailed as possible. This is to reduce the time to think about what the goal is. This must answer the basic questions of Who, What, When, Where, Which and Why. The more specific the goal, the more the end result can be envisioned by the goal setter. This corresponds into the sports theory that an athlete can see the goal before it is attained through training. Studies have affirmed that visualization helps immensely in the attainment of a desired goal.

Measurable – When setting goals, it must be specific that progress can be held up against a measure, or a benchmark. In bodybuilding, it is measurable to state that the goal is to bench press a weight of 200 pounds in two months' time. The old adage states: "if it can be measured, it can be attained" is also a known fact among athletes. Athletes keep a record of their performance, on and off the field, in order to have something to compare against. They even measure other athletes in different sports to improve their understanding.

Attainable – This is a part where you determine the will to reach your goals. Do you think the goal is attainable? Will it help you fulfill your overall goal? The more specific a goal is, the more you can find ways of reaching your target. You develop and educate yourself on reaching those goals.

Realistic – Does it make logical sense? Getting to Mars and back within 20 days is a goal, but with the resources you have, is it realistic? Will it take a huge effort to achieve the objective? A person must be willing and especially able to achieve the goal. It is still realistic to aim high. It has to do with the rewards received, or the way the goal moves you forward. If

Creating Goals

you don't possess the skills or inclination to reach the goal, then the goal is unrealistic. No amount of motivation can get a man to do what he despises.

Time-bound – This is the most important of all. A goal has to have a deadline. This is to prevent the goal setter from letting his goal slide from one day to the next. The true price paid for goals is the time you give the goal. For example: "I will lose 10 pounds by January 1, 2017, which is three months from today."

The key to a life of continual learning and improvement lies in developing a specific plan for growth and following through with it. Once you have set your goals, you need to create a plan.

The process of personal growth planning revolves around the creation of an action plan that is based on your ambitions for development in areas such as career and education, but also self-improvement. In general, the plan contains a statement of a future reality and the way you intend to realize it.

Most people are facing difficulties when it comes to the question what they should include in their personal growth plan. Very broadly, your plan should contain the following five criteria:
1. What you want (or where you want to be).
2. Why you want it.
3. How you plan to accomplish this vision.
4. The potential obstacles, risks and dangers.
5. How you plan to overcome the difficulties.

You can also include alternative plans that you can quickly execute in the case of failure. It can be beneficial to thoroughly answer the following questions, before developing the plan:
- What do I really want to make out of my life?
- What kind of a person do I really want to be?
- Do I have a vision of what I want to see implemented in this world?
- What are my goals and ambitions?
- What are my dreams?
- Are my current decisions leading me exactly where I want to be?

Planning isn't difficult. What is difficult, though, is creating a plan that will actually get you where you want to be. This also means that you will have to identify everything that will get you closer to your goals.

The 4-1-1 on Reinventing You

This is what you need to do in order to specify your individual growth plan:

1. **Taking of an inventory.** Evaluation might be the most difficult part of creating your personal growth plan. It requires you to be honest with yourself and the situation you find yourself in. The analysis of your current situation helps you to identify the areas that you can work on in the future. This stage also requires you to reevaluate your goals and ambitions.

2. **Writing of a mission statement.** Having a personal mission statement can be helpful to people who want to be able to evaluate the purpose of their actions and activities. Such a statement helps you to ask yourself if whatever you are doing contributes to your mission or not.

3. **Short and long-term planning.** When developing a personal growth plan it is crucial to separate your plans into short, medium and long-term sections. If you are only planning in the long run, you will most likely neglect the importance of planning of short-term actions.

4. **Reassessing your plan.** The continuous reassessment of your plan allows you to develop responses to recent developments. It will further help you to make better decisions at the present moment.

5. **Committing and taking action.** What is the purpose of having a plan if you do not execute it? To make sure that you don't forget your plan, be committed to it and take the action that is necessary to implement it.

Your personal development plan should also detail how you plan to improve in different areas. You can consider the following learning opportunities:
- Courses
- Workshops
- Reading/Literature
- Mentoring
- Networking
- Training on the job
- Joining groups

Creating Goals

There are many more ways to gain exciting new skills. Let's continue with some examples.

Personal Development Plan Examples

A personal growth plan can be broken down into the following areas:

1. What do I want to accomplish in life? What's the true purpose of my life? The importance of knowing what you were born to do should not be underestimated. It gives you the necessary foundation on which you can build your plans for the future. However, discovering your life's purpose is a complex process which takes time. (Example: It is my vision to help create a better world by making the world's knowledge easily accessible for every human being.)
2. What are my dreams? We all grew up with the most ambitious dreams, only to lose sight of them once we grew older. Don't make the mistake of rationalizing the very dreams away that inspire and motivate you.
3. What kind of a person do I really want to be? What are my beliefs and values? Ask yourself what it is that you stand for—the beliefs you hold and the values you appreciate.
4. Who am I now and who do I want to be in the future? The analysis of who you are at this present moment, and the person you want to be in the future, helps you identify areas to work on.
5. What are my goals? Don't underestimate the importance of having realistic but inspiring goals. These goals should, preferably, be separated into short, medium and long-term goals. A short-term goal has, at times, been of approximately half a year. Medium-term goals approximately 1 to 3 years and long-term goals 5 years or more.
6. What are the necessary milestones? Many people only focus on the setting of ambitious goals, without realizing the importance of also specifying the necessary milestones they need to accomplish. Having milestones allows you to break a goal down into several sub-goals. Doing so will allow you to maintain the necessary motivation, even when you are working on a long-term goal.

Remember this: Time is the true price paid for your dreams. The earlier the dream can be achieved the more time you have to enjoy it. Don't let other people rob you of your goals. Use the SMART method and share it with others so you can help each other reach your goals.

The 4-1-1 on Reinventing You

Self-Discovery Challenge:

Complete each type of goal for the following focus areas: *Career, Education, Finances, Self-Improvement, Social, and Mind, Body & Spirit.*

Short-term goal

My short-term goal is:

It is important to me because:

Current factors impacting and/or relevant to the goal include:

. . . . **Creating Goals**

My timeline is:

The strategies I've already implemented towards this goal include:

People (family, consultants, coworker, or friend) who can help me stay on track are:

The 4-1-1 on Reinventing You

Medium-term goal

    My medium-term goal is:

    It is important to me because:

    Current factors impacting and/or relevant to the goal include:

. . . . **Creating Goals**

My timeline is:
The strategies I've already implemented towards this goal include:

People (family, consultants, coworker, or friend) who can help me stay on track are:

The 4-1-1 on Reinventing You

Long-term goal

My long-term goal is:

It is important to me because:

Current factors impacting and/or relevant to the goal include:

. . . . **Creating Goals**

My timeline is:
The strategies I've already implemented towards this goal include:

People (family, consultants, coworker, or friend) who can help me stay on track are:

Chapter Eleven

Words Create Realities

• • • • • • • • • • • • • • • • •

"In the beginning was the Word, and the Word was with God, and the Word was God."
—John 1:1

We could all learn something from this well-known Bible verse. Looking beyond the religious overtones, there is a message to be found in this for everyone – everything begins with a word.

> **Everything begins with a word.**

Words consist of vibration and sound. It is these vibrations that create the very reality that surround us. Words are the creator; the creator of our universe, our lives, our reality. Without words, a thought can never become a reality.

This is something that we have been taught throughout history, as far back as the Bible, which writes of 'God' – whatever that word may mean to you – saying 'let there be light' and as a result creating light.

So what can we learn from this? If our words and thoughts are the very tools with which we create our reality, then surely they are our most powerful tool yet? Surely we should only pick the very best words in order to create our very best reality?

Our thoughts also impact what we manifest in our lives – but it can be argued that the real power lies within our words. It is our words that

The 4-1-1 on Reinventing You

provide a bold affirmation of our inner most thoughts. They are a confirmation to the world of how we see others, our lives, and ourselves. It is this powerful affirmation that our words provide which enables our thoughts to manifest into a reality.

So why do we choose to misuse our most powerful asset? As a society, we have become conditioned to talk about our misfortunes and problems. We take our interpretations of events, people and ourselves and communicate them to the world – bringing them into existence.

So by that admission, when we moan or complain about our lives to others, we are putting those negative words out there to become a reality. When you say something out loud enough times your words become the truth not only in your own mind, but in the minds of everyone you are saying them to. If this is really so, ask yourself – do you really want to tell yourself and everybody that you know that you are unlucky in love/unsuccessful/miserable/bored or whatever you have been complaining about? Especially now that you know that it is these exact words that are creating the life that you live?

Begin to choose the words that you speak consciously. Practice improved self-awareness over the words that you use to describe yourself and your life. Negative, powerless words such as "can't", 'shouldn't", "need", "won't" should all be avoided – they strip you of your ability to manifest a life that you want to live.

As the creator of your universe – what you say goes. Therefore, next time you catch yourself about to use negative words, regain control and frame your word choices so that they have a more positive impact on your world. For example, if you would usually say something such as "I am unhealthy and overweight" then why not turn this into a more positive, constructive statement such as "I am in the process of becoming healthier and every day I get closer and closer to my ideal weight".

Your words are the paint with which you paint your reality. Choose them wisely and positively to create a reality that is good for you.

"I Am What I Am"

Affirm who you are, your dreams, your hopes and your successes with two of the most powerful words that a person can ever utter – "I am".

These two small but incredibly powerful words should be considered the most precious words that you have in your entire vocabulary. How we end the sentence "I am..." defines who we are to ourselves and to every-

Words Create Realities

body around us. So, when you say "I am...fat/lazy/shy" or "I am...beautiful/confident/successful/happy" this is the exact truth that you are creating for yourself. It doesn't even matter if there is any truth in the words that you are saying, how you finish those two little words is how you define your reality.

So why not choose a higher expression for yourself? Remind yourself of what you are and what you wish to be by starting each morning with a positive affirmation beginning with those magical words "I Am." (*More on Affirmations in Chapter 12"*)

Speak from the Heart

When we complain about our life; speak anxiously or use hateful words; we usually do so from a place of fear. So, the first step that you need to take in order to conquer this is to practice better self-awareness over the words that you are using.

Next time you open your mouth to complain or put yourself or others down, ask yourself, "why am I about to say this?" and "how is this going to serve me or my happiness?" Ask yourself these two important questions and you will no doubt discover that you are in fact speaking out of fear – the fear that you are not good enough, fear that you are in the wrong relationship, the wrong career etc.

> **Always speak from a place of love; for yourself, for your life and for others.**

Most importantly of all, you will realize that by voicing these fears you will be doing nothing for your happiness. Your words can only make you feel worse, manifesting these fears into your life with greater intensity.

So choose your words bravely, consciously and lovingly. Always speak from a place of love; for yourself, for your life and for others. Your words equal your world, so use them wisely.

Your thoughts have real substance, although your scientific instruments can't yet measure them. You might imagine your thoughts as "magnets." These "magnets" go out into the world and attract the substances that match them; they duplicate themselves in form. Everything around you was a thought in someone's mind before it existed in your

The 4-1-1 on Reinventing You

reality. Cars, roads, homes, buildings, and cities all existed as thoughts before they became realities

Your thoughts set up the model of what is to be created, and your emotions energize your thoughts and propel them from your inner world to your outer world. The stronger your emotions are, the more rapidly you create what you are thinking about. Your intent acts to direct your thoughts and emotions, maintaining a steady focus on what you want until you get it.

Because your thoughts set up the model of what you draw to you, it is important to think about what you want rather than what you don't want. You will not get what you want by fearing or hating its opposite. For instance, having money does not come from disliking living in poverty. Whatever you focus on is what you get, for energy follows thought. The more you love having money and abundance, the more you picture it and thus draw it to you.

It is also important to think in positive ways. Positive emotions and thoughts draw what you want to you. Negative emotions don't bring what you want; they bring only what you don't want. Spend quiet, reflective time thinking positively about what you want. When you don't think in higher ways, dwelling on things such as problems, you repel abundance.

Don't feel bad about the negative thoughts you have, for fearing or disliking your negative thoughts gives them more power. Respond to negative thoughts as you would to small children who don't know any better; simply smile and show them a better way to be. If you recognize a negative thought, simply place a positive thought alongside it. If, for instance, you catch yourself saying, "I don't have enough money," simply say "I have an abundance of money."

Positive thoughts are far more powerful than negative thoughts. One positive thought can cancel out hundreds of negative ones. Your soul stops your lower and negative thoughts from becoming realities unless having them manifest will teach you something that will help you grow. You are loved and protected by your soul and the universe. As your thoughts become higher and more positive, your soul allows more and more of them to manifest. The more you evolve, the more power your thoughts have to create your reality, and the more responsibility you have to think in higher ways.

. . . . **Words Create Realities**

There are many wonderful tools you can use to learn to think more positively. For instance, you can put light—an image of physical light—into the pictures in your mind. You can practice making negative thoughts fade out or dissolve, and lighting up positive thoughts. Take a moment right now to think of something you want. Select one thought you have had about why you CAN'T have it. Now, imagine that thought fading out, or imagine that thought written on a blackboard that you are erasing, or imagine putting that thought in a balloon and letting it float away. Do whatever motivates you to remove that thought from your reality. Now, create a thought about why you CAN have it. See that thought written out; put white light around it. Imagine someone reading the thought to you in a beautiful voice. Create a mental image of receiving or having what you want. Make the image so real you can almost touch, smell, see, and feel it. Make the image bigger, so that you are standing in the image rather than just observing it.

By making your negative thoughts fade out, you take away their power to create your reality. By making your positive thoughts more vivid and real, you increase their ability to create what you want. There is great power in repeating the thought of something you want over and over. When you've received something you wanted in the past you probably thought about it frequently. Repetition firmly implants the idea of what you want to create in your subconscious, and it goes about bringing you what you think about. You want the thought to be definite and unwavering.

The biggest reality of all — Stop "Should-ing" yourself

We all say it – "should have," "could have," and "would have." But just how many times do we say them a day? Every day we act, feel, and do things that feel right for us then question them because these things go against the course of what others feel and think. We love a certain type of music, yet if it is not the most popular kind we immediately start off with "I know it's stupid, but I just love this band."

Our favorite past time is sitting outside reading a good book instead of partying all night so we immediately start our sentence with "I know I am a dork, and it is so weird, but I actually love just reading and being outdoors." Or, we fall head over heels in love with someone who does not necessarily reciprocate those feelings so instead of showing our vulnerability and allowing ourselves to give love even when it is not returned, as if it's not ok, we say "I know I shouldn't feel this way towards them and I am trying not too…."

The 4-1-1 on Reinventing You

We constantly deny our true feelings and thoughts out of pure acceptance from what the so called "norm" is, which ends up leaving us feeling confused and frustrated as to why we do feel a certain way, or do certain things when we "should" feel different. We end up feeling insecure because we have convinced ourselves that it's not okay to feel whatever we feel instead of just letting go of the idea that we must handle each scenario in life exactly as everyone else does. Or we hold to the notion that we must like and do things exactly as others, instead of realizing that we have our own voice and feelings that are purposeful to life as a whole.

As I started to take inventory of the most important aspects of my life—my marriage, my family, my friends, my health, my work, my spiritual practice, my finances, and more—I was a bit stunned to realize that much of my motivation in these key areas comes from the perspective of what I think I "should" do, say, or feel, and not from a place of what's authentic and true for me.

As I look more deeply at this within myself, I realize that my obsession with doing, saying, or feeling the way I think I should be, is actually less about a desire to do the right thing and more about fear, shame, and a lack of self-trust. When I operate from that place of "should," it's often because I'm feeling scared, flawed, or simply not confident in my own thoughts and beliefs. This insecurity leads me to look outside of myself for guidance, validation, and the insatiable right way something should be done—which is often stressful, anxiety-inducing, and damaging.

> **When I operate from that place of "should", it's often because I'm feeling scared, flawed, or simply not confident in my own thoughts and beliefs.**

What if instead of asking ourselves, "What should I do?" we asked ourselves different, more empowering questions like, "What's true for me?" or "What am I committed to?" or "What do I truly want?" These questions, and others like them, come from a much deeper place of authenticity and truth.

Words Create Realities

This is not to say that everything we think we should do is inherently bad. Thinking that we should do things like eat better, communicate with kindness, exercise, follow up with people in a timely manner, spend time with our families, take breaks, save money, have fun, work hard, be mindful of the feelings of others, push past our limits, try new things, organize our lives, take good care of ourselves, focus on what we're grateful for, and so much more—all can be very important aspects of our success and well-being, as well as that of those around us.

However, when we come from a place of should, our motivation and underlying intention for doing whatever it is we're doing is compromised—even if it is something we consider to be positive or healthy. In other words, we often feel stressed, bitter, resentful, worried, or annoyed when we're motivated by should. This "should mentality" is based on an erroneous notion that there is some big book of rules we must follow in order to be happy and successful.

The distinction here is one of obligation versus choice, or "have to" versus "get to." When we stop "should-ing" on ourselves, we're less motivated by guilt, fear, and shame and can choose to be inspired by authentic desire, commitment, and freedom.

Here are a few things you can do to stop "should-ing" on yourself:

1. **Pay attention to how much "should" runs your life.** Take some inventory of your life, especially the key areas and relationships, and notice how much of your motivation is based on "should." You may even notice how often the word itself comes out of your mouth in relation to your own actions and thoughts or conversations about others. The more you're able to notice this, without judgment, the easier it will be to alter it.

2. **Play around with different words, thoughts, and motivations other than "should."** If it's not about what you (or others) "should" do, what are others words, thoughts, or motivations you could have? How can you relate to the most important areas and people in your life differently? Inquire into this and see what comes up. It's not simply about word choice (although words do have a great deal of power), it's about altering where you're coming from in a fundamental way.

The 4-1-1 on Reinventing You

3. **Ask yourself empowering questions.** As I mentioned above, instead of asking yourself the question "What should I do?" see if you can ask yourself more empowering questions—ones that lead you to an authentic and inspired place of motivation.

Here are some as examples:
a) "How can this be fun?"
b) "What would inspire me?"
c) "What's in alignment with my mission?"
d) "How can I serve?"
e) "What would make me feel good about myself?"

There are so many possibilities, once we let go of "should."

Words Create Realities

Self-Discovery Challenge:
List alternate words for the word "should."

Think of things you "should" do or be doing and replace the above words in those sentences. How does it change your attitude about doing them?

The 4-1-1 on Reinventing You . . . .

How we end the sentence "I am..." defines who we are to ourselves and to everybody around us. Finish this sentence: I am...

Enlist a partner to keep you honest about your "should". List the name of the person below and the date/time you will enlist their help.

Chapter Twelve

Affirmations and Visualizations

* * * * * * * * * * * * * * * * *

"Belief consists in accepting the affirmations of the soul; unbelief, in denying them."
—Ralph Waldo Emerson

Is it possible to work in the course of self-development by using visualizations and affirmations?

Yes, it's possible to use visuals and affirmatives to manipulate through self-development. Since self-development is a lengthy process, it is always nice to have our mental capacity and capabilities assisting us along the way.

> **Imagine it, amplify it, and imprint it on your mind. The results will amaze you.**

It is vitally important that you can clearly visualize the reality you wish to create. The higher the detail of your visualization, the deeper the impact will be on your subconscious mind. It is important that you visualize every detail you possibly can, especially feelings, emotions, and

The 4-1-1 on Reinventing You

sensory perceptions. What will it feel like to achieve success? Imagine it, amplify it, and imprint it on your mind. The results will amaze you.

As human beings, we are highly influenced by habit: habit of action, habit of thinking, and habit of belief. It is these habits which are the driving force in how we shape our reality. Visualization is a very powerful tool that will prepare your mind for success. The more you visualize that which you want – the more aligned your thoughts, beliefs and actions will be – and this will ensure you manifest the reality you desire.

Still, we need support and help from others. It is always nice to have friends that share similar qualities as yourself. It gives you inspiration, so you don't feel as if you are in this huge world all by yourself. Having people around you with parallel interests, differences, and characteristics is part of self-development. This is because influences reflect on how we cultivate our skills and abilities.

We need to set goals and make plans for an easier life. Organization skills and other human developmental skills are required. We learn from the inner self. The inner self is our director, thus the one in charge that carries us through the self-development phase.

Most people don't recognize that naturally we all develop to certain levels. Since influences factor into our development, we see that it could create problems. Problems could develop, such as bad habits, behaviors, thinking and so forth. This is often true when we associate with people that think negative and reflect their thinking on us. Our behaviors are persuaded by influences.

Visualizations and affirmatives can help you develop that higher plane of consciousness and self-awareness. You reap benefits, since while you are in the process of developing your skills, you will also build emotional competency. This process of development is highly essential, given that emotions for centuries have gotten many people in a world of trouble.

Since the world is changing toward technology, the Internet is encouraging young adults to go online and play games to build their visualization and affirmative skills. The games accessible have proven to assist some children with developing self-awareness while putting the emotions at ease.

If you struggle with the self-development process, perhaps you can join the online gamers and take advantage of the new age resolutions for self-development. Surely, you know however, that games are not the

Affirmations and Visualizations

sole invention that we must use to navigate through the process of self-growth while using affirmation and visualizations.

In fact, it takes more than games to develop a single human being. What it takes is time, practice, preparation and willfulness. Time, preparation and practice in this order, collective with willingness, will encourage you to stay focused on the subject. You want to keep your goal in mind by using visualizations. We can find many benefits while working through our self-development in a logical order.

Affirmations are acknowledgments of the inner self, which gives one inspiration to move ahead. The affirmatives give us the aptitude to assert and defend our intentions. Affirmations help us to corroborate authentic messages that one can verify. Affirmatives are statements that come from our reports, speech, actions and so on. It allows us to build endorsement so that we can work toward our goals. For example, an affirmation might be "I'm a good problem solver and people always look to me for answers to their problems."

Visualizations are mental images that we conjure up in the mind. It gives us a clearer picture of what we are thinking, or what others are saying to us. When we develop mental pictures in our head it can give us new ideas, or help us develop new ideas. We create dreams through mental pictures, which also help us to develop new ideas.

Mental images are often created through brainstorming or meditation. When we brainstorm or meditate while conjuring up mental images, it inspires the mind. We develop plans, and design from this action. Moreover, we can take initiative action by picturing in our mind what we must do.

Visualizations help us to use thought to consider our beliefs, views, opinions, theories, concepts and so forth. We can use visualization and affirmatives for developing the inner self. Self-development starts in the womb, and carries forward throughout the direction of one's life. We all have several ways to further visualization parallel to promoting our capability to employ affirmatives through meditation.

> We all must give the mind room to breathe so we can think positive in order to profit from visualizations and affirmatives.

The 4-1-1 on Reinventing You

Meditation can assist you with pulling your mind together to start visualizing the self in a scene of position, space and time. Meditation encourages relaxation, which helps you to stick to moderate plans while working through self-development. It will turn out to be easier for you.

Relaxation eases your mind; thus it helps you to take up again creating mental pictures in your mind so you can start thinking optimistically. We all must give the mind room to breathe so we can think positive in order to profit from visualizations and affirmatives.

Self-growth is a process that allows us to use affirmations and visualizations in order to manipulate through the procedures. Affirmatives and visualizations are encouraged in college and have been used to assist individuals with developing a positive mind. Positive thinking assists one with the process of self-development by giving courage. From beginning to end, mental pictures have been widely used as enforcers.

We all have to work our way through self-development. Despite where we pick up and move faster to develop our skills, we all have to get it done. Sadly, however, many people have left the world underdeveloped, and many more will leave the world the same way. Many people miss the benefits of meeting the inner self. The inner self is the entire being within each of us that sets us free from burden, distress, illness and other harms. We have the inner strength, which is the inner self that allows us to draw from its source, to find ways to develop the entire human being.

Yet, we have many things to consider. We have to discover our self-identity throughout the process of development. Online you will come across hints that will help you work through self-development by using affirmatives and visualizations. Many hints offered for self-development today are directed toward the new age arena. We are in the new age now, so why not explore the market to see what is happening. Take the tips and use them to your advantage.

We have the best of both worlds with affirmations and visualizations, since the two tools can help us reach out above our limits and go beyond our future. Using these tools, we can build on our future by applying the positive learning from our mental creations.

· · · · · · · · · · · · · · Affirmations and Visualizations

Self-Discovery Challenge:

Writing an affirmation letter can assist in generating the focus and details needed to create a new reality. You can use letters or just one or two sentences. The key to affirmations is to repeat, repeat and repeat. Write yourself an affirmation letter on something positive in your life.

The 4-1-1 on Reinventing You

Write down what your ideal day would look like from sunrise to sunset.

. . . . **Affirmations and Visualizations**

Write a letter to yourself explaining why it has been hard to achieve a goal. You might be very surprised about what comes out.

The 4-1-1 on Reinventing You . . . .

What one or two sentence affirmation sticks with you that you will repeat each day to yourself? (For example: "I have total control over my visualizations;" or "I use the power of visualization to manifest the life I want;" or "My mind is focused and clear when I visualize.") Search the Internet for affirmations if you need inspiration. Write your affirmation(s) down below. Remember to post each one everywhere you can see it and repeat several times each day.

Chapter Thirteen

Networking and Social Media

> *"It occurs to me that our survival may depend upon our talking to one another."*
> —Dan Simmons

Whether you're transitioning from online relationships to in-person ones or starting completely from scratch, there's a lot to know about networking. And if you're heading to your first in-person event without so much as a user's manual, well, you're in luck.

In-Person Networking

Here's a survival guide for your first in-person social networking event:

Yes, you'll need to talk with strangers. Sounds scary, I know. But you may actually find a few new friends in the group, even friends who end up in the life-loyal category. But to turn strangers into friends, you'll need to learn how to talk to strangers, how to start, maintain, and end a conversation with style. The ability to focus on a specific conversation point with someone makes us memorable and establishes commonality. Ask people about what they do, interesting trends they see in their industry, and the values and fundamentals you believe you have in common.

The 4-1-1 on Reinventing You

Come with business cards. Often a common sign of a new person is the lack of a business card. Can you get by without one? Sure. But it feels good to have one, and it also helps all the new people who are exposed to you that day remember you. A good networking business card looks professional and includes key data about you and your life or business objectives.

Practice your elevator pitch. Not everyone loves the idea of the elevator pitch. The elevator pitch is a 20 second bio of yourself and what you do, or have to offer. To some, it feels like a tired exercise. But like it or not, you'll be asked to tell your story in some fashion during a networking event, so you should come prepared.

Mistakes to avoid. Remember: It's not all about you. Don't come overdressed. Don't over-distribute your business cards. And, don't act with selfish abandon.

Make a memorable impression. A firm handshake, a warm smile, a hug, a shared laugh, an unexpected conversation, a personal connection established with an initial meeting—these are all things that can only happen in person.

Arrive early and stay late. There are many benefits to this tip. First, you won't be late. That means you can relax, find the room, and scope out the layout. Second, you can connect first with the speaker (if there is one) and the event leadership, introducing yourself and perhaps getting a few tips on who will be there. Finally, staying late allows you to maximize your time away from home. After all, you already took the time to get dressed and drive over.

Know your objectives cold. The most common question at a networking event is, "What are you looking for?" Do you know the answer? Be specific. Your answer to this question will either help people place you in a category for sharing job leads or leave you in the corner with others who were vague. Give specifics, including at least a few target qualities.

Don't sit until it's necessary. Nothing says, "don't come talk to me" like taking a seat. It says you're done for the day/night when you should just be getting started. Have you ever been in a conversation in which information that has not yet become common knowledge in your industry is revealed? People tend to reveal this kind of information in intimate face to face conversations. This can happen in part because of the sense of trust that is established in the moment. When it comes to business and career opportunities, amazing info is shared in person that is NOT shared elsewhere. So don't sit until it's necessary.

Learn about people's back stories. Everyone has a story that can reveal so much about where they come from, how they have gotten to their current place, and what common ground you can find with them. We all share human experiences in business. These experiences have taught us all the importance of hope, hard work, and faith to help us through.

Introduce people to each other in person. Not everyone is comfortable chit-chatting and small talking with others at networking events. Take the opportunity to introduce people to each other when you believe they might be a good fit. This includes businesses that may be complimentary, personalities that match up, or just cool people that you feel should know each other.

On-line Networking

The days of in-person networking are quickly being overpowered by connecting on the internet. In the past five years, connecting on social networking sites has rocketed from a niche activity into a phenomenon that engages tens of millions of internet users. Now, instead of connecting at an in-person event, you can reach hundreds, even thousands, of potential customers online. Social networking can help you reach new markets and enhance your customer service.

Don't let the fact that you don't yet know the person hold you back from sending an invite to connect. Simply be transparent, and let them know why you'd like to connect with them online. Whether you're offering your help, sending them a resource or introducing them to one of your connections, make sure you make it about how you can help them and not how they can help you.

Social media's value for brand-building, sales, and customer engagement is regularly discussed and debated. But one area that's frequently overlooked is its incredible networking ROI (Return on Investment), especially for introverts who may not want to attend large, noisy professional gatherings.

Networking through social media is a great way to build up your professional contacts and is essential to growing your network. Nearly everyone has a social outlet they use regularly. Finding and connecting

The 4-1-1 on Reinventing You

with influencers on those outlets gives you both a chance to get to know one another without the hard sell.

Networking is an ongoing process, but each key person in your network can change your future. Take time to find that person today!

Groups and discussion areas on social sites are all over the internet from LinkedIn and Xing to Twitter and Facebook. Most social networking sites have community areas for people who have similar interests to gather and connect. It's important to find a dozen or so of these groups and discussion areas and not only join and monitor them but engage in the conversations as well.

Blogs are another type of discussion forum on the internet. Blogs are quickly becoming places to interact with your target market. Technorati, a site focused on helping people find great blogs and content specific to their industry or topic, manages a list of the top 100 blogs, which is a great place to find the world's most popular blogs on subjects you're interested in. Not only can you find connections and blogs on this site, but you can also list your own blog so that people can search and find you.

With any social media platform, you need to be creative and find ways to provide value and engage your target market. One of the best ways to accomplish this and position yourself as an industry leader, is to build and launch a Facebook fan page. Fans are enthusiastic, and if they like what they see and read, they'll connect with you, become loyal supporters and tell their friends. This is how word-of-mouth will grow.

Once you get your fan page up and running, pay attention to your analytics, or what Facebook calls "Insights." You can view specific demographic information, such as where your fans are from, their gender and their age. Monitor who's becoming your fan, how they're interacting and how often they're posting. This will help you figure out who and where else you should be targeting online.

One of the main differences between a Facebook profile and a fan page is you can send bulk messages to all your fans. You can also "Suggest to Friends" that they join you on your fan page. It's a great way to connect with your target market, especially since these are connections that have opted-in to become a part of your community.

So whether in-person or online, put yourself out there. It only takes one great connection to get the word out on the services you provide or what you have to offer.

Networking and Social Media

Self-Discovery Challenge:

Master the 20-Second Pitch – You only have a few seconds to wow someone!

What if you just entered an elevator and recognized someone you have been trying to get in front of for what feels like an eternity? What would you say?

Before you dive into the actual pitching, take these factors into consideration:

1. What are your most valuable assets?
2. Which type of person should you approach? Contacting online customers is different than pitching face-to-face customers, so create a pitch generated toward specific audiences.
3. Be the expert in your field.
4. Think like your customers in order to deliver what they want. Research your customers to know what they want.
5. Be prepared to have multiple pitches for different customers and their level of expertise.

When conversing with potential customers, time is at a premium. Don't be slow to get to the point. Lead with the obvious – who you are and why you are calling or speaking to them. The order of your presentation is important, and there will be times you won't have time to spit out many details. Think in terms of hooks, buzz words, bullet points, and headlines. You want to be perceived as serving their needs.

The 20-second pitch (or Value Proposition Statement) amounts to around 100-120 words. Use them wisely. Write out your pitch to see its length and begin to replace words that shorten sentences. Switch out other words for impact. Give your first name when speaking and don't worry about your last name – most don't remember it anyways.

The 4-1-1 on Reinventing You

VALUE PROPOSITION TEMPLATE

The value proposition template breaks down your statement into five simple parts: (1) Identify, (2) Audience, (3) Your unique solution, (4) the Transformation, and (5) the "How" that will follow by engaging with your message. Here's how they work together:

1. I AM _____

This is where you spell out your professional identity. Answer the question: Who are you? Because that's what your customers want to know. (State your first name only at this point, along with your credentials.)

2. I HELP _____

This is where you identify your target audience. You can make an educated guess here, but to really dial it in and find out who your audience is and what they need, I recommend conducting a reader survey. You can also ask friends and those close to you.

3. DO OR UNDERSTAND _____

This is where you spell out your unique solution to your customer's needs. Most of our solutions come down to empowering or informing in some way. Use an action verb to capture empowerment – I've used do here, but it could be anything: find, regain, experience, and so on. To capture the informational, try verbs that deal with revelation: understand, see, etc.

4. SO _____

This is where you sell the transformation. Help the customer see what your solution can do for them. After all, that's why they're coming to your site or business to begin with. Remember: you are solving a problem here.

5. I DO THIS BY (or THROUGH) _____

This is where you explain how you will accomplish what you are proposing.

Here are two examples:
"My name is Sam. I'm a blogger and speaker who helps weary adoptive and foster parents find the support and validation they need to regain hope and finally stop feeling alone. I do this through my online programs and speaking content."

. . . . Networking and Social Media

"I'm Nancy. I am a technology and lifestyle coach. I design custom productivity systems for successful but overwhelmed business leaders, so they can regain a sense of control and focus on what matters most. I do this by offering 1:1 coaching and online programs."

You can see how the five elements of the template come together to make a powerful value proposition, giving you – and your customers – the necessary clarity to skyrocket your impact.

Now it's time for you to write your Value Proposition Statement.

I AM _____

I HELP _____

DO OR UNDERSTAND _____
_____
_____
_____

SO _____
_____
_____

I DO THIS BY (or THROUGH) _____
_____
_____
_____.

The 4-1-1 on Reinventing You . . . .

How have you used social platforms to start a conversation?

What networks have helped you build your circles and make connections?

Search the Internet for Social Media Platforms. Sign up for a new one today. Get connected. Write the name of the new network.

Chapter Fourteen

Transformation Requires Self-Care

• • • • • • • • • • • • • • • • •

*"We do not need magic to transform our world.
We carry all of the power we need inside ourselves already."*
—J.K. Rowling

Most of my lifetime has been spent trying to please and take care of others. I never realized that if I didn't take good care of myself, I wouldn't be able to take care of my family. Taking time out to do something for yourself doesn't make you a selfish person, regardless of what others say. You have to have peace of mind to concentrate on the tasks at hand. If you are overwhelmed and don't take a time out, your work and family life could suffer. You don't have to spend a lot of money to have time to yourself. Reading a magazine on the patio away from everyone works well. Go for a walk. Take a bubble bath. Just make sure to allow the same courtesy to your partner. He (or she) needs time too.

Me, Myself, and I:
- Although it is very important to devote time to your relationship, time for yourself is just as important.
- Take care of yourself first and everything else will fall into place. If you are not well, you cannot take care of others.

The 4-1-1 on Reinventing You

- The old saying "if mom is not happy, no one is happy" is pretty much true! So take time for you.
- Be true to yourself.
- Love yourself. Love yourself. Love yourself.
- Be yourself no matter where you are.
- Be confident in everything you do.
- There is no shame in getting professional help if you feel overwhelmed or depressed.
- Your car, home, and job do not define you. You define you.
- Get a manicure, pedicure, or massage when time and your budget permits. Or, get together with a friend and give each other a manicure or pedicure.
- Get your yearly medical exams and blood work done.
- For women: do self-breast exams once a month. Ask your doctor to show you how.
- When you get stressed out, ask yourself if it will matter in five years. If the answer is no, let it go. If it is yes, find a solution.

Character Traits:

What character traits do you want to possess? Good personal character traits will better your chances of success in achieving your goals in both your personal life and your professional life. Good social character traits result in other people wanting to do business with you or to have personal relationships with you.

Below are some personal trait guidelines

- Temperance – Avoid excessive food and drink.
- Order – Organize your time effectively and keep all things in their place.
- Resolution – Do what you resolve to do without fail.
- Frugality – Spend only what benefits yourself and others and waste nothing.
- Moderation – Avoid extremes and forgive injuries. Injuries refers to an injury caused by another, whether physical or emotional—don't indulge your resentment.
- Industry – Be diligent and use your time productively.
- Cleanliness – Tolerate no uncleanliness in the body, clothes, or home.

Transformation Requires Self-Care

- Tranquility – Don't sweat the small stuff. (And, it's all small stuff.)
- Humility – Imitate Jesus and Socrates.
- Sincerity – Be fair in thought and word.
- Silence – Speak only to benefit yourself and others.
- Justice – Do no harm and do your duty.
- Chastity – Keep your lust in check.
- Morals & Values – Establish the morals and values of how you want to live your life. Associate with those that share these and remove yourself from the company of those that don't.

We must consider those genetic traits, such as eating disorders and drinking alcohol in excess, which may pose difficulty in the temperance guideline. However, it does not mean a person fails to follow the above guidelines. After all, no one is perfect.

The 4-1-1 on Reinventing You . . . .

Self-Discovery Challenge:

From the list under Me, Myself and I, what are some of the items you can start doing today?

What character traits to you currently have?

What new character traits do you want to incorporate into your daily life? (Trait, Date/Time to incorporate)

Conclusion

When it comes to trying to find the answers inside yourself, you have to dig deep into your soul and your mind to find the right answers you are looking for. It is a long process and no one will tell you that it's easy, yet you can accomplish much by putting forth effort.

5 things to have clarity for change:

1. Know what you want. Don't just understand what you don't want. Work toward something with the reinvention in mind. Don't just simply run away from something else.
2. Get clear on what you want and why. Then when you get it. You will want what you have.
3. Don't feel the need to justify your move. If someone is curious about your "why," tell him or her in simple and truthful terms. No one can argue with the facts. He may have opinions, but the five minutes he spends thinking about you is nothing like having to live your life 24 hours a day.
4. Find others. Get in touch with a coach, mentor, or someone who has transitioned from one thing to another. Such people are available more places than you would think – and more people are wanting to reinvent themselves than ever before.
5. Take action. Every day you spend in stagnation is one less day you'll spend in success. Small deliberate steps add up. Take one today.

The 4-1-1 on Reinventing You

There are simply too many people looking at reinvention as a risk, when it is an opportunity with a poor name tag. Instead of asking yourself, "What should I do?" consider asking yourself, "What do I want to get out of what it is that I do, or I'm good at?"

To get started, you have to be able to take a long look inside yourself, which is not easy for anyone, but in order to be able to find answers it has to be done. This is where a Life Transformation Specialist can help you.

A Life Transformation Specialist and a Certified Personal Coach helps you to search your mind and insight to help you find your hopes and dreams, as well as to feel motivated enough to make your wishes come true. This is all about finding yourself and helping you to have better insight of yourself.

It takes some time to become someone in a professional stance but as you grow, you will find that it will be easier for you to handle your responsibilities. This will help you to be able to define who you are and what you want in life. The process will help you to become a successful businessperson, as well as a successful individual. In order to become a professional, you have to work at it. This is not going to be something that doesn't take any time or effort; this is going to be an ongoing effort.

People will experience hard times, but you will learn how to overcome this and walk through it. You will not only cross over discrepancy, but you will come across many self-emotions and experience the power of self-growth. You will feel anxiety, fear, resentment, guilt and a lot of uneasiness. However, when you are feeling this way, the professional help you seek will assist you in learning to overcome it and move forward.

How does one get on the right path? It will all depend on you and your frame of mind, on how fast you will progress. It is going to take some time but as you learn to work on it, it will come to you faster than someone who only thinks they want it. The transformation process will help you to go deep inside of your thoughts and feelings. Throughout the process you will create goals, both short term and long term. These goals, once down on paper, become real. You will place these goals in front of you so can see them and read them each day to keep your mind fresh. The more you see and read something the more it will become "real." In order to become the success, you want to be, there is work that you are going to have to do.

What if you write it down and it doesn't happen? The first thing to stop and consider is, maybe it did happen, just not the way you intended. Go back and look at the outcome, the benefit of the benefits. What was it you

. . . . Conclusion

wanted out of that goal or dream? You may have gotten what you wanted after all, just in a different way.

If you feel you aren't ready for a coach or specialist, begin your self-development through studying and reading at the library, or read in a quiet place in your home, so that you have a peaceful environment for learning. There should be no noise to get you sidetracked while you are working. Just keep heading in the right direction. Keep walking and keep on writing it down to make it happen.

Utilize the Self-Discovery sections of this book to guide you in the direction of your reinvention.

Find your solutions. Take Action Today!

Resources

Maxwell, J. (2016, April 19). *Blog*. Retrieved from John Maxwell: http://www.johnmaxwell.com/blog/

Sfakianos, M. (2015). *Building Leadership through Self-Insight*. Open Pages Publishing, LLC.

Sfakianos, M. (2016). *National Association of Christian Women Leaders*. Retrieved from NACWL Blog: https://www.nacwl.com/category/michele-sfakianos/

Takeactionwithmichele.com – My website is dedicated to personal life transformation, speaking and training for individuals, families and businesses in areas such as: Leadership, Parenting, Communication, Personal Growth, Finances, Team Building and more.

Twelve Time Management Habits by Benjamin Franklin, one of the Founding Fathers of the United States [World Wide Web]

Wikipedia 2016: https://en.wikipedia.org/wiki/Law_of_attraction_(New_Thought)

Index

A

Affirmation(s), 59, 78-79, 87, 89-91, 93-94
Affirmative(s), 87-90
Anxiety, 58, 82, 108
Attitude, 20, 51-54, 85

B

Belief, 10, 19, 27, 36-37, 69, 82, 87-89
Benefits, 47, 55, 88-90, 96, 104, 108
Bible, 77
Blog, 47, 98

C

Certification, 30, 33
Challenge, 6, 13, 21, 23-28, 33, 38, 40, 50, 55, 62, 70, 85, 91, 99, 106
Character traits, 104, 106
Clarity, 101, 107
Coach, 101, 107-109; *see also* *Life Transformation Specialist*

College, 29-32, 90
Comfort zone, 23-25
Confidence, 15-20, 26-27, 53
Connect, 7, 36, 96-98

D

Declutter, 43-50
Degree, 30-31, 33

E

Education, 17, 30-32, 67, 70
Emotional baggage, 48, 50
Emotions, 17, 61, 80, 87-88, 108
Empowering, 82, 84, 100

F

Facebook, 12, 46, 98
FAFSA, 30; *see also Loan*
Faith, 51, 57, 59, 61, 63, 97
Fear, 2-4, 16-17, 35, 48, 57-63, 79, 82-83, 108
Feelings, 48, 81-83, 87, 108
Frustrated, 3-4, 10, 47, 57-58, 82

The 4-1-1 on Reinventing You . . . .

G

Goal setting, 24; *see also Goals; Long-term goal; Medium-term goal; Short-term goal*
Goals, 9, 11, 19, 22, 24-25, 31, 35, 40, 65-69, 71, 73, 75, 88-89, 104, 108
God, 5, 58, 61, 77
Grateful, 38, 48, 51-53, 55-56, 83
Gratitude, 51-55
Group, 68, 95, 98
Growth, 19, 36, 59, 67-69, 90; *see also Personal growth; Self-growth*

H

Habit, 3-4, 9, 11, 24-25, 39, 44, 61, 88
Healthy self-esteem, 15-16
Hobby, 25, 46

I

Impression, 18, 96
Influence, 11, 24, 88
Influencer, 98
Internet, 31, 88, 94, 97-98, 102

J

Jesus, 58, 105
Journal, 26, 56

K

Kindness, 5, 83

L

Law of attraction, 52

Leader, 98, 101
Leadership, 36, 96
Life Transformation Specialist, 108
LinkedIn, 98
Loan, 30
Long-term goal, 69, 74; *see also Goal setting; Goals*
Low self-esteem, 16

M

Magnets, 79
Market, 19, 90, 97-98
Meditate, 10, 59, 89
Meditation, 10, 59, 89-90
Medium-term goal, 69, 72; *see also Goal setting; Goals*
Memorable, 95-96
Memorable impression, 96
Mentor, 20, 35-39, 41, 107
Mindful, 44, 59, 83
Mission statement, 68
Mistakes, 15-16, 37, 96

N

Negative thoughts, 17-18, 20, 22, 52, 80-81
Negativity, 59
Networking, 68, 95-99, 101

O

Objectives, 19, 36, 96
Obstacles, 20, 24, 67
On-line, 97
Over-inflated self-esteem, 16

P

Passion, 1-2, 6, 26, 36
Pell grant, 30; *see also Loan*

Index

Personal development, 68-69
Personal growth, 36, 59, 67-69; *see also Growth*
Physical environment, 44, 47
Positive thoughts, 20, 80-81
Program, 2, 4, 30-32, 46, 100-101
Purpose, 1-5, 7, 9, 45, 58, 68-69

Q
Quiet, 26, 65, 80, 109

R
Realistic, 24, 66, 69
Reality/Realities, 11, 59, 67, 77-81, 83, 85, 87-88, 91
Reinvention, 36, 107-109
Relationships, 2, 9, 16-17, 47-48, 83, 95, 104
Relaxation, 90
Resentment, 48, 53, 104, 108

S
School, 20, 29-34, 46, 48
Self-care, 44, 103, 105
Self-Discovery, 6, 13, 21, 28, 33, 40, 50, 55, 62, 70, 85, 91, 99, 106, 109
Self-esteem, 15-16, 20, 27
Self-growth, 90; *see also Growth*
Self-improvement, 27, 67, 70
Self-talk, 15, 17, 19-22
Short-term goal, 22, 69-70; *see also Goal setting; Goals*
Should-ing, 81, 83
SMART, 66, 69
Social media, 3, 12, 95, 97-99, 101-102

Solutions, 100, 109
Strangers, 2, 25, 53, 95
Strengths, 26, 36-39, 59
Stress, 43, 58
Success, 3, 10, 18-19, 23, 27, 35, 44, 47-48, 78, 83, 88, 104, 107-108
Successful, 19-20, 23, 35, 37, 79, 83, 101, 108

T
Temperance, 104-105
Thoughts assessment, 20
Tranquility, 105
Transformation, 2, 48, 100, 103, 105, 108
Twitter, 12, 98

V
Value proposition, 99-101
Value(s), 5, 37, 46, 69, 95, 97-101, 105
Visualizations, 87-91, 93-94

W - Z
Weaknesses, 26, 37-38, 59
Xing, 98

MICHELE SFAKIANOS (Sfa-can-iss) is a Registered Nurse, Certified Life Transformation Specialist, Speaker and Trainer. She is also a Leading Authority on Life Skills and Parenting, and an Award Winning Author.

In 1982, she received her AS Degree in Business Data Processing/Computer Programming. In 1993, she received her Associate in Science degree in Nursing from St. Petersburg Junior College, graduating with Honors. In 1999, Michele received her Bachelor of Science degree in Nursing from Florida International University, graduating with High Honors. Michele received her John Maxwell Certification in Coaching, Speaking and Training in 2015.

Michele is the owner of Take Action with Michele, Inc. and is also the owner of Open Pages Publishing, LLC. Her first book "Useful Information for Everyday Living" was published October 2010 and was later changed to "The 4–1–1 on Life Skills" and released June 2011. Her other books include: "The 4–1–1 on Step Parenting," released October 2011; "The 4–1–1 on Surviving Teenhood," released October 2012; "Parenting with an Edge," released June 2013; "Teen Success: It's All About You! Your Choices – Your Life," released June 2013; "Building Leadership through Self-Insight," released October 2015; and "Parenting Plan; Preparation is Key," released November 2015. Michele has also written two children's books: Aaron's Special Family and Aaron Bug.

Open Pages Publishing, LLC

Open Pages Publishing is a self-publishing company offering books to inspire, teach, and inform readers. We specialize in a variety of subjects including: life skills, self-help, reference, parenting, and teens.

Ordering Information:

Open Pages Publishing books are available at online bookstores. They may also be purchased for educational, business, or promotional use:

- For bulk orders: special discounts are available on bulk orders. For details contact our sales staff at info@openpagespublishing.com.

If you would like to receive an autographed copy of this book or other books published by the author, please email the following information to info@openpagespublishing.com:

- Full Name
- Address (street address, city, state, zip, country)
- Phone Number (including area code)
- Indicate which book(s) you are interested in:
    - *The 4-1-1 on Life Skills*
    - *The 4-1-1 on Step Parenting*
    - *The 4-1-1 on Surviving Teenhood*
    - *Parenting with an Edge*
    - *Teen Success: It's All About You! Your Choices – Your Life*
    - *Ace Your Life*
    - *Building Leadership Through Self-Insight*
    - *Parenting Plan – Preparation is Key*
- Name of the person the book should be autographed to
- Indicate if for a special occasion (birthday, anniversary, graduation)
- Payment methods include Visa, MasterCard, Discover, American Express, and PayPal.

VISIT MY411BOOKS.COM

Made in the USA
Columbia, SC
16 August 2017